In this insightful book, Merrel
Path of Assurance"—a practic
ing God's will. If you want to
in your life, *It's Not Complicated* can help.

—Jim Daly
President, Focus on the Family

Merrell McIlwain has distilled decades of experience struggling to know God's will into the book you are holding. But you will not find a formula to follow. As you will see, God's will is more personal than solving a spiritual equation. May these pages be like a loving friend who sits beside you, encouraging you every step of your journey to the will of God.

—Chris Fabry
Author and Host of Chris Fabry Live on Moody Radio

All of us at various points of our lives long to know God's will. Merrell's book is many years' lived experience, solidly biblical and highly practical! I have no doubt it will be useful in your life's journey as well!

—Dr. John Fuder
Moody Bible Institute, Together Chicago

In my opinion, a book about the will of God in your life should not be theoretical. I believe Merrell writes from a life that has embraced, lived, demonstrated and values discerning and doing God's will. This is the one book that you and I must have in our hands and pass on to our children, who will pass it on to their children.

—Martin Simiyu
Executive Director, Possibilities Africa

If you are longing to know God's will for your life, this book will awaken some fresh biblical ways of seeing how God has been working in your life. It is a practical guide that will cause you to delight even more in the Lord's will. And, it is not as complicated as you think. This is a must-read!

—Frank Holsclaw
Pastor Emeritus, Pawleys Island Presbyterian Church

You got me when I was an unformed youth, God, and taught me everything I know. Now I'm telling the world your wonders; I'll keep at it until I'm old and gray.

—Psalm 71:18 (MSG)

IT'S NOT COMPLICATED

A Practical Guide to Experiencing God's Will

Delight Yourself in the Lord !

Merrell McIlwain

MERRELL MCILWAIN

Paperback ISBN 978-1-960007-40-7
eBook ISBN 978-1-960007-41-4

Published by
Orison Publishers, Inc.
PO Box 188
Grantham, PA 17027
www.OrisonPublishers.com

Contact the author at:
Merrell S. McIlwain II
3811 Thistleberry Road
High Point, North Carolina
Phone: (719) 337-9657
Email: merrellcheri@gmail.com
www.merrellmcilwain.com

CONTENTS

PREFACE

W hat is God's will for my life?" I have wrestled with that question since junior high school. At that time I was trying to figure out where I should go to college. I didn't understand who I was trying to please or why, the factors I should consider, or what my choice might eventually mean. Like most of my friends, I was pretty much clueless.

I needed a dependable way to make decisions, but I didn't know what that should be. So I put a lot of effort into finding the answer to my question. Over the years I read the Bible and other books, talked with my friends and pastors, prayed for guidance and even taught some classes about how to find God's will. Finally I graduated from Moody Bible Institute with a degree in Biblical Studies.

But I still couldn't be sure of the answer. There was never enough time for me to consider all the facts before it was time to act. The books I read were sometimes contradictory or too complex for me to follow, and the answers the authors proposed didn't seem to work anyway. I knew God was a key part of the process, but I was never sure what He wanted me to do.

That is why I have written this book. Now, at more than seventy years old, I have the perspective to explain a practical way that you can experience God's will. I call it "The Path of Assurance." It is energizing and allows you the freedom to enter the open and spacious life God has promised to you and me. As you read this book, be open to new ideas about the age-old question, "How can I understand and experience God's will in my life?"

My special thanks go to Dr. Marilyn Cassis of Charleston, West Virginia, a good friend who suggested I write a book sharing my beliefs and experiences. I also greatly appreciate the many friends who talked with me about how God has worked in their lives. I could never have completed this book without the wise counsel, expertise and guidance of Chris Fabry and Keith Carroll. And last, but not the least, I want to mention my special and lasting love and thanks to my wife, Cheri, whose encouragement, proofreading and assistance were critical to the completion of this book.

INTRODUCTION

You have been created with the obligation and ability to grow and learn as a child of God and, as you do, to more fully resemble Him.

Therefore, God's will for your life is not difficult to find. God doesn't hide His will under an invisibility cloak or require you to follow a complex path to find it. Instead, the first step in experiencing God's will is simply delighting yourself in the Lord. When you do that, God will give you new desires to serve Him.

As you recognize those new desires, you must take action. God has given you judgment and wisdom, which you should use to make day-to-day decisions. God will work them all into good while conforming you to the image of Christ. With God ensuring that all things work together for good, you can make choices freely. As you do, God will provide you with the confidence to take the next step, and the next, and the next.

Then, instead of asking God to show you His will, you are free to simply do His will. The end result will be bigger, bolder and better than anything you could ever imagine, and it will take you places you never dreamed as God does the impossible. This book focuses on life in the here and now, and how you can experience the will of God to become more like Him.

Chapter One

THE SEARCH

Now unto him that is able to do exceeding abundantly above all that we ask or think...

—Ephesians 3:20 (ASV)

D oes God really have a plan for you and your life? If He does, why is it so difficult to find? Do life's answers seem hidden? Do you feel confused or hopeless at times? Has the search for God's will left you feeling trapped, waiting until you're certain before you act?

If the answer to any of these questions is yes, there is good news! God's will is not complicated. It is much simpler and easier to find and follow than you have been told. God is not hiding it. Why would He? He wants you to thrive and live a life overflowing with His love.

Is God's will mysterious? Is the path to finding it long and hidden? It is not!

I want to simplify your search and help you understand God's plan for your life. I'll provide tools needed for finding and tracking God's will. You will see events in your life in a new way and find opportunities that are bigger, better and bolder than you thought possible as God fulfills His promise to provide you with a free and open life.

1

That's my hope for you as we begin. My prayer is that you will discover what God has in store for you and how you can experience it!

God's Will

Have you ever thought about doing something that seemed impossible? For me it was a visit to Asia. When I was only eight years old, we moved to a house with a big yard. I was sure that if I could dig a hole deep enough, I would come out in China. However, there were many mistakes in my thinking. I didn't know that I would have to dig more than 12,000 miles or that the deepest hole ever dug was only 7½ miles deep. Nor did I know that I would run into super hot magma when I reached the center of the earth. I simply had a shovel and a dream. So when I got home from school, I headed to the backyard. I dug and dug, day after day, only to be frustrated by the rocks and roots I encountered. After several afternoons of work but only a few feet of progress, it finally dawned on me that my plan was impossible. Eventually I also learned it was the Indian Ocean, not China, that was on the other side of the world.

Have you ever felt that way about God's will? You want to find it, but you have no idea how, or how long it will take, or where it might lead you. Some of the things you might have heard are these:

- God's will is almost impossible to find. It's like walking a tightrope or looking for a needle in a haystack.
- God's will always leads to something that will make you miserable.
- Finding God's will is like walking blindfolded with your arms outstretched, hoping you won't trip and fall.
- You must wait until you hear a clear, precise call from God in order to truly do His will.

Do you see how these thought patterns can lead to confusion and frustration? You might as well be trying to dig a hole to Asia, right?

But finding God's will is possible. This book is subtitled *A Practical Guide* because it is not about the theory of God's will, but about how to find His will in real situations. It explains how to make sensible decisions freely and without fear. Instead of considering God's sovereign will or moral will, it simply explains how to find what God wants you to do now.[1] That is, it helps you find God's individual will for you and your life. This book is based in part on my experiences, and it begins there. I am not a famous person with a dynamite story to tell; instead, I am sharing what has happened to me throughout my life because it illustrates how you can experience God's will.

Personal Experience (Part 1)
My life began in the hills of West Virginia, in the small town of South Charleston, where my dad was a teacher who became a high school principal. My mom, while also having a degree as a teacher, stayed home to take care of me and my two younger sisters, like most of the other mothers in our neighborhood. In fact, only 7 out of about 150 students in my elementary school had special permission to bring their lunches because their mothers worked. The rest of us walked home for lunch every day. There was no lunch (or breakfast) program at school; those were much simpler days.

We were a strong Christian family, like most of the families in our town. My parents taught me right from wrong and were hard workers who demonstrated lives of integrity. When the church was open, we were there—for Sunday morning church services, Sunday evening vespers and youth fellowship, Wednesday night prayer meetings, covered dish dinners and other events that inevitably came up. You get the idea: it wasn't just about looking good at church; instead, faith was a key part of our lives.

My dad was superintendent of the junior high department at church (with about 120 kids), and my mom was a Sunday

---

1 The "sovereign will of God" refers to God's predetermined plan for what happens in the universe. It is certain and will be fulfilled, but it does not violate human responsibility or make God the author of sin. It is hidden from discovery and is perfect, working all things together for God's glory and humankind's good. God's "moral will" refers to the commands in the Bible that teach us how to live and includes principles to guide our lives. It is God's individual will for each of us that is the subject of this book. See Garry Friesen, *Decision Making and the Will of God*, rev. ed. (New York: Multnomah Publishing Company, 1980, 2004), Chapters 2 and 12.

school teacher. The scope of my mom's Bible knowledge was amazing. For example, when I was about three or four years old, she made me a little coat, following a pattern she bought and then made with her sewing machine. She said that she was inspired by the Old Testament story of Hannah in First Samuel 2:18–19 who made for her son, Samuel, a little coat each year. I heard this story and many others over and over as a young boy, and they changed my life.

I was baptized as an infant, publicly professed my faith at age eight, and was president of our high school fellowship. I also memorized the children's catechism, and I have always believed the Bible is God's true and infallible word to us. I believe Jesus was born as God incarnate, died for my sins and was physically resurrected as a foreshadowing of what is promised to every believer. From my earliest memories I had dreams that there was more to life, and I wanted to see and experience new things—to become part of something bigger than myself. I knew that with our family's financial situation, however, going out of state for college would be impossible.

When I was in seventh grade, my dad was invited to go with a group of West Virginia educators to visit a new college in Colorado Springs, the United States Air Force Academy. He came back with pictures and stories about what sounded like exactly the place I had been dreaming of, with new facilities, dorms, athletic fields and much more. Its literature also advertised that if you attended, you would become a part of the aerospace team. I didn't really understand what that meant, but somehow I knew it would be great. The education would be excellent, and it was all cost-free, with room, board and classes all included.

Instead of paying tuition, graduates were required to serve in the military for at least five years. That seemed even better; it was free and I was guaranteed a job when I graduated. From then on I dedicated myself to the goal of getting a congressional appointment and becoming an Air Force Academy cadet. Upon graduation from high school and after years of writing to my congressmen, studying and getting into physical shape, I was accepted as one of about 1,200 cadets into the class of 1972.

At that time the United States military academies admitted men only, so it was difficult to meet women. Some cadets had girlfriends back home, but everyone else, including me, was anxious to meet local women. Since we were limited in being able to leave the campus during our first two years, the best way to meet someone was to await the arrival of buses on the weekend from women's schools in Denver. The women would stay for a few hours and then go back on the buses to their schools. There might only be sixty who would arrive, and they would be faced with a couple hundred cadets hoping to meet them. It seemed impossible.

But then one of the best things that could have happened did happen. My roommate, who lived in Denver, was dating a young lady from a nearby college, and he was helping her organize a get-together for cadets and some of the women from her college. My roommate asked if I and several other cadets might like to go. Did we want to go? Was he kidding? Of course we wanted to go! Later that night at an amusement park in Denver I met the lady who turned out to be the love of my life, Cheri. There will be more about her later. But for now, suffice it to say that she was beautiful, vivacious and for some reason thought I was fun to be with. We started dating and quickly fell in love, but students couldn't be married while attending the Academy.

After graduation we got married and moved to Nashville, Tennessee, where I enrolled in law school at Vanderbilt University. She was a speech-language pathologist working in the public schools, and consequently she was able to quickly get a job anywhere we lived. Three years later I graduated, and we headed to our first Air Force assignment near Champaign, Illinois, followed by our second assignment, which was back to teach at the Academy. As my military service commitment came to an end, I applied with law firms in Denver, Colorado, (where Cheri was from) and my boyhood home of Charleston, West Virginia. I followed the then current (but now outdated) practice that included mailing printed résumés, responding to phone calls and having in-person interviews. I received offers from firms in both cities and had to decide what to do.

I was young (thirty-one years old), inexperienced and naïve when we had to make our decision. I wanted to follow God's will, but I had very little idea how to go about that. We made a pros and cons list about where we might go and what I would do in the various jobs. This decision was complicated by the fact that I tended to keep my thoughts to myself and then announce my decision. On the other hand, Cheri rightfully wanted input, and so there was conflict that neither of us liked.

As the time for a final decision approached, we chose a career in Charleston, West Virginia, in one of the largest law firms in the state with more than 200 employees. At the law firm I quickly learned there would be long hours and difficult assignments. I arrived first to start work and the family followed in a few weeks. Much later Cheri told me that as she got on the plane leaving Colorado with our kids, she was sobbing as she said goodbye to her family and home state.

Every attorney hired hopes to become a partner, which means you have an ownership interest in the firm. With this your income begins to skyrocket and you soon become very wealthy. The partners bought new cars every couple of years, had big houses and took frequent vacations to exotic places! After four years I became a partner and it seemed to be a dream come true for me at age thirty-five.

Soon, though, I began to realize something was wrong. I can vividly recall that despite working from 7:00 a.m. until 5:30 p.m. Monday through Saturday, I still had to return to work after dinner. I had fallen into a pattern of leaving the office in time to get home for dinner where I would eat and talk with my wife and kids for a few minutes. Then at about 7:00 p.m. I headed back to the office for a couple more hours.

Our kids were at the age when they couldn't bear to be separated from me and my wife. They could easily get homesick at summer camp or even when visiting a friend overnight. Of course we loved them, too, and tried to maximize our time with them. On those frequent nights when I had to go back to work, I would hug and kiss them and tell them "good night" because they would be asleep when I got home. As I was leaving I would look back at the house and see the kids' little faces pressed up against the front window waving goodbye. That is one of my most lasting and painful memories. I knew this couldn't be good for our family, but I didn't know what to do about it. The common statement among the other attorneys on Fridays was said jokingly, but I learned it was true: "Well, only two more workdays this week."

I was working more than I ever intended, and it wasn't doing our marriage or my parenting any good. I was frequently so tired and stressed out that I would be short-tempered and irritable. But was I free to just leave? What about God's will in all of this? We had made a decision to live and work in Charleston, so maybe I should just stick it out and hope things might get better. Or maybe I should consider a new job, but what would that be?

By this time I knew that I had to be more intentional about seeking God's will, although I still didn't know how to find it. I did know the lifestyle that had at first seemed so attractive was beginning to look empty. But how could I know if it was God's will to leave the firm and take another job?

I had to find out quickly, while also thinking about the needs of the family. Things were difficult and confusing. If I found God's will, how would I know for sure? What did the Bible teach? I was hoping to be led like Abraham or get some sort of a sign, but I didn't really know what to expect—especially under such pressure. Should I talk to others, seek a miracle or what? How could I think it through clearly enough to ever make a decision consistent with God's plan for my life? I had so many questions. One of the first things I needed to know was whether I could find another job. I began talking with a "head hunter" in New York who helped me find a legal position available with a large company in Birmingham, Alabama.

I continued to pray about what I should do and to read the Bible regularly. I talked with a few friends, many of whom thought I would be crazy to leave the firm after becoming a partner. Cheri, though, had an aunt and uncle and six cousins who had lived in Birmingham a few years before. She had visited them every summer for years, so she felt somewhat comfortable with the location.

I talked with a very helpful Christian counselor who said I was right to consider options both in Charleston and elsewhere. He thought the transition would not be as difficult as I anticipated. I also discussed it with my grandfather. He was then ninety-one years old, on his way to a life of 101 years. He said something that really surprised me; he told me I was "so young I could try several different jobs." By then I was thirty-five years old and thought I was too old to be changing jobs, but he had a different perspective.

My wife and I also were influenced by the writing of Dr. James Dobson with Focus on the Family. He spoke about the dangers of constantly devoting your life to power and money while losing things much more important: your family and ultimately control of your life.

All the advice was good, but it didn't point me in any one direction; in fact, it seemed contradictory. Both doors seemed open, and we didn't experience peace or get a clear answer to the question about God's will.

Still not sure what to do, I felt like:

- I might be stepping off a cliff and was filled with fear because it would be a long fall if I made the wrong decision;
- I would never get the chance again to make so much money;
- I had proved myself at the firm and might fail in a new position; and
- It would be crazy to leave our established life in Charleston and move to the unknown city of Birmingham with all that would involve for me and the family.

Finally, despite our fears and the concerns about the move and not being sure about God's will, because time with the family was most important, we decided to leave the firm and move to Birmingham. I was one of the few partners who had ever left the law firm. The process, however, took months and caused conflicts with my wife (who got tired of listening to me), my parents (who didn't want me to leave), and my friends (who had mixed messages). I never knew if I heard from God or was just hoping I would. As we moved to Birmingham, we wondered whether we had found the will of God or if we had accidently gotten off track.

That was probably the hardest decision I ever made. It was hard not because it was the biggest or most important one, but because it was the first time I understood we were making a decision that would forever change the future for me and the family. It wasn't an easy or simple thing to do. We didn't fully grasp what had happened until several years later.

Decisions, Decisions, Decisions

You will make thousands of decisions throughout your life. The impact of some will be felt for years to come; others will be quickly forgotten. There will be big decisions—what to study, who to marry, how many children to have, where to live—and less important ones—what to wear, whether to buy a car, what cell phone company to use. You will have to make some right away while others allow you to have more time. But one thing is true: the next decision is never far off.

To be sure that you act within God's will, you would prefer to wait until you have heard clearly from Him. But you realize that if you wait too long, something will happen anyway, so you must make your decision now. The next decision won't be far behind, and this process will be repeated over and over during your life.

When facing a major decision, God's will becomes the question you wish you had resolved when things were normal—not when you are facing a big decision. Suddenly finding God's will moves from the sidelines to the front and center in your thinking. My friends who are pastors tell me the same thing; they are usually asked about God's will when someone is in the midst of a life-changing decision. But wouldn't it be best to consider the question, "What does God want me to do?" during the calm before the storm of the next big decision, a storm you know is coming?

It's Not Too Late

God has provided us with the promise of living a free and full life of energy and strength. In Second Corinthians 6:11–13 Paul writes,

> *Dear, dear Corinthians, I can't tell you how much I long for you to enter **this wide-open, spacious life**. We didn't fence you in. The smallness you feel comes from within you. Your lives aren't small, but you're living them in a small way. I'm speaking as plainly as I can and with great affection. **Open up your lives. Live openly and expansively!*** (MSG, emphasis added)

And in Ephesians 1:16–19 he says,

> *...I ask—ask the God of our Master, Jesus Christ, the God of glory—to make you intelligent and discerning in knowing him personally, your eyes focused and clear, so that you can see exactly what it is he is calling you to do, grasp the immensity of this glorious way of life he has for his followers, oh, the utter extravagance of his work in us who trust him—**endless energy, boundless strength!***[2] (MSG, emphasis added)

It is not too late for you to find and experience God's will. You haven't missed it because of something you did or didn't do last month or years ago! And you don't have to follow an intricate process to be sure you have found His will, or go to a foreign country as a missionary, or wait for a miracle. When you place your faith in Jesus and His finished work on the cross, He can and will use you—wherever you are and whatever you are doing—to accomplish His will. You are ready and able to fulfill God's will for your life right now.

The truth is that God's will is wonderful and not hidden. You can find and follow it while living a life filled with joy and boundless strength. In this book I will introduce a new and different way of

---

2 Psalm 37:39 says, "The spacious, free life is from God, it's also protected and safe" (MSG).

looking at this question. I call it "the Path of Assurance," and it will allow you to make decisions freely and with confidence. It has worked well for me and allowed me to experience an expansive life filled with the energy promised by God. I believe it will do the same for you, too!

Heavenly Father,

Thank You for who You are, the Creator of all people and all things, and the God who loves and cares for each of us. We praise You for sending Your one and only Son, Jesus, to earth to live and die and through His death and resurrection to forgive and redeem us. As a result of Your grace, we now stand justified before You and will live forever in Your presence. How can we ever thank You for this immense gift? We pray that You will open our hearts and minds and allow us to see how and where we might serve You. Let us more clearly understand Your will for our lives and be open to a new way of experiencing it. We ask You to guide and bless us now and throughout our lives.

We pray this in the name of Jesus, amen.

Chapter Two

DELIGHT YOURSELF IN THE LORD

His delight is in the law of the LORD, and on his law he meditates day and night.

—Psalm 1:2 (ESV)

L aw firms are often structured on a pyramid model. At the bottom are the mail clerks, copy assistants and other support people. Next come the secretaries, then the paralegals and then the associate attorneys. At the top of the pyramid are the partners, the attorneys who own the law firm. Although everyone else in the pyramid is paid a salary, the partners divide the profits among themselves. This is done according to the percentage assigned each of them by a "shares committee," and some partners get more than others.

At one particular firm the shares committee was made up of three members at the very top of the pyramid. Bryan was one of them, and he was also one of the most highly regarded banking attorneys in the state. On a beautiful Sunday afternoon while at his summer cabin on the river outside of town, Bryan, age sixty, unexpectedly dropped dead of a heart attack. After a few days of hushed reverence and fond memories retold about Bryan, the tone quickly changed. Throughout the firm other attorneys began vying for Bryan's status and possessions: his corner office with its luxurious furnishings, his cases and client list, his reputation as the best banking lawyer, and, most of all, his place on the shares committee.

One day Bryan was literally on top with power, possessions and status that few ever experience; less than a month later he was little more than a footnote, rapidly forgotten as the practice returned to "normal" and life rushed on without him. It is a lesson that I never forgot about the brevity of life and our worldly accomplishments.

How can you find meaning and know what is most important? How can you be certain that your decisions are consistent with God's will for your life? Having wrestled with those questions for more than seventy years, I believe there is a straightforward answer.

It is called the Path of Assurance, and with it there are two—only two—Bible verses necessary to experience God's will. The first of these is Psalm 37:4, which says, "Delight yourself in the LORD; and He will give you the desires of your heart" (NASB).[1] In this chapter we will look at the first part of that verse, which is the first step in experiencing God's will for your life.

Psalm 37:4a
Delight Yourself in the Lord

What does Psalm 37:4 mean when it says, "delight yourself in the Lord"? Could you just say a quick prayer affirming your love for God? Or is there something more to it? To figure out that answer, begin by asking yourself this question: what do you truly delight in right now? Is it money or fame? Could it be a better position, or multiple homes, or living at the beach? How about music, travel or having a healthy body? Any of these and many others could be your delight. These are the things you plan for and think about most.

Consider what Paul teaches:

---

1 The context for Psalm 37 is the conflict between the wicked and the righteous, in which God assures the righteous that they will prevail. He also assures the righteous of several blessings, including in verse 4 that God will grant them the desires of their hearts. A similar thought is in Proverbs 16:3: "Commit to the Lord whatever you do, and he will establish your plans" (NIV). See also John Mac Arthur, *Found: God's Will* (Colorado Springs, Colorado: Cook Communications Ministries, 1998).

...Train yourself for a holy life! While physical train-ing has some value, training in holy living is useful for everything... (1 Timothy 4:7–8 CEB).

...pursue righteousness, holy living, faithfulness, love, endurance, and gentleness (1 Timothy 6:11 CEB).

So then, let's work for the good of all whenever we have an opportunity (Galatians 6:10 CEB).

As Paul tells us in Galatians 5, "Christ has set us free for free-dom...You were called to freedom, brothers and sisters; only don't let this freedom be an opportunity to indulge your selfish impulses, but serve each other through love...the fruit of the Spirit is love, joy, peace, patience, kindness, goodness, faithful-ness, gentleness, and self-control" (verses 1, 13, 22–23 CEB). Paul encourages us to grow in our relationship with God and human-kind. Our time on earth allows us to refine ourselves as we devel-op in the image of the Lord.

Instead of seeking more, think about what God has already done. Think about the fact that there is order and predictability in the universe and about His moral laws[2] that separate us from animals and provide a way of right living. Think about the other blessings, things like a place to live, work and serve; your fam-ily; your health; and the other things you enjoy. Over time you will experience a sense of peace, of love and wonder, and a joy in knowing that you are blessed to be a blessing. As you thank God for what He has done for you and ponder your blessings, you will experience a gradual change in what brings delight.

Keeping your focus on the Lord takes effort, but it will become part of the growth you experience over the years as you find ever-in-creasing satisfaction in the truths of God. Commit to reading God's Word, obeying His moral laws, praying, being in fellowship with other believers, meditating on God's goodness, and loving others.

---

2 God's moral laws are intended to bring you "into a proper relationship with God and regulate your conduct toward orderly and beneficial living" (*The Daily Bible* NIV, Commentary by F. LaGard Smith [Eugene, Oregon: Harvest House Publishers, 1984], 210).

Galatians 5:22–23 (MSG) explains that God brings delight into our lives in the same way fruit appears in an orchard. It is a slow process that happens over time as seeds grow into plants, develop blossoms and eventually produce fruit. In Philippians 2:13 we read, "For God is working in you, giving you the desire to obey him and the power to do what pleases him" (NLT). When you begin to delight yourself in the Lord, you will see things begin to change. You don't have to wait until you become less sinful; you can start now.

Other issues will still be there, but God begins to take first place. As you love and serve God, you will find new and improved delights in your heart—joys that can only come from God. In Philippians 3:4–11, Paul tells us he considered his prior accomplishments to be garbage compared with the joy of knowing Christ. As he put his trust in Jesus, he was radically changed from being self-focused to becoming God-focused.

In the 119th psalm, the psalmist finds delight in the law of the Lord. As you read that psalm you notice that he first reads and studies God's Word to be sure he understands it, then he follows God's laws as best he can.[3] Psalm 119 paints a picture of someone who doesn't look for parts of the law he can avoid or find a way to get around. You can become that kind of person! And in Ephesians 4:24 we read, "And then take on an entirely new way of life—a God-fashioned life, a life renewed from the inside and working itself into your conduct as God accurately reproduces his character in you" (MSG).

Professors call this process "progressive sanctification," which means after you become a Christian you begin to learn and apply more and more of God's teaching in your life. And as you grow, you begin to more fully understand the importance of the role and power of the Holy Spirit.[4]

In the New Testament book of Philemon we learn that a man named Philemon had become a believer in Christ after hearing

---

3 "Keep company with God, get in on the best" (Psalm 37:4 MSG); "...to love the Lord your God, to walk in obedience to him and to hold fast to him" (Deuteronomy 11:22 NIV).

4 Similarly, Psalm 1:1–3 reads, "Blessed is the one who does not walk in step with the wicked or stand in the way that sinners take or sit in the company of mockers, but whose delight is in the law of the Lord, and who meditates on his law day and night. That person is like a tree planted by streams of water, which yields its fruit in season and whose leaf does not wither—whatever they do prospers" (NIV).

Paul preach in Ephesus. Philemon was the owner of a bondservant, or slave, who had escaped to Rome.[5] That slave, Onesimus, had no thought about whether his escape was right or wrong, and he certainly was not planning to ever go back to his former owner. But later while in Rome, Onesimus heard Paul preach and became a believer. He then found what brought him delight was changing. He wanted to make things right with Philemon, but under Roman law there were stiff penalties for runaway slaves.

Paul wrote a letter to Philemon asking for his forgiveness and acceptance of Onesimus. He said, "For this perhaps is why he was parted from you for a while, that you might have him back forever, no longer as a bondservant but more than a bondservant, as a beloved brother..." (1:15–16 ESV). Paul's request not only brought the two of them together, but it also gave Paul the opportunity to teach Christians what it means to be one in Christ. This shows that as you delight in the Lord, your circumstances often expand, and the result is usually unexpected.

There are some people who read Psalm 37:4 but move through the part about delighting in God quickly, not giving it much thought. They are far more interested in God fulfilling the desires of their heart. So you might wonder, "Could I wait to delight myself in the Lord until after I get the desires of my heart?" The first part is not optional, however, and it must be done before God will grant the desires of your heart.

This is often challenging because you probably know what you want. Perhaps it is a new car, or a better job, or clarity about who to marry, or what to do next—the list is endless. And you want those things right away! So it is tempting to skip the first step of delighting yourself in the Lord and move quickly on to the second. But you must first take delight in Him.

The process does not happen overnight, but as you delight in God you inevitably become a new and different person. In *Sharper Eyes of Faith,* the author says, "So by personal, intimate, spiritual time with God in worship of Him, His desires become [your] desires. [You] can bask in sweet communion with Him, allowing

---

5 Bondservants were people sold into servitude for a specific number of years and in that respect differ from what most Americans think when they hear the term "slave."

His desires to become [your] desires. Here is real contentment!"[6] In other words, as you honor and worship God alone, you find God is much more concerned with who you are and your relationship with Him than in what you do for Him.[7]

Unresolved Questions
There are many questions about God's will. These can easily confuse your search and lead to erroneous conclusions. Some of them are set out here, and the answers will be explained throughout the book.

- Why does the Bible not provide a specific way to find God's will? It provides detailed discussion of Christian liberties; roles in the church; spiritual gifts; love for one another; how to behave in church; how to receive communion; prayer; resolving disputes; relationships between husband and wife, parents and children, as well as between employers and employees; what constitutes sin; marriage and sexual matters; how to treat others; and on and on. Why is the question of God's will not mentioned? Why is direct discussion of this important topic not included?
- What about big versus small decisions? Although most commonly thought about in the context of life-changing decisions, some people look for God's will in all matters, no matter how insignificant, such as what kind of soup to buy.[8] Where do you draw the line between big and small decisions, like what to eat for breakfast, or when to go to the store, or the dozens of other minor decisions you make each day? What if two believers are facing the same decision, but one considers it to be a less important matter and the other sees it as very important? Is one of them right and the other wrong? Is there any way to know?
- What about believers who are young? What do you tell them about God's will? Imagine a child who professes

---

6 Harry Stephen Hager, *Sharper Eyes of Faith: A Widower's Journey* (Llano, Texas: Equipped Mama, 2022), 111.
7 Oswald Chambers, *My Utmost for His Highest*, August 4 (Grand Rapids, Michigan: Discovery House Publishers, 1992), 158.
8 Charles F. Stanley, *The Will of God: Understanding and Pursuing His Ultimate Plan for Your Life* (New York: Howard Books / Atria Books, 2019), 104-5.

his or her faith in Christ and is facing an important decision. Maybe it is how to respond to others at school who are bullies, or how much of the allowance to give to the church, or when to get a license to drive. There are big decisions in young lives, but do we take them seriously and talk about how these young people should approach the question of finding God's will? At what age should children start to seek God's will? In the many books I have read on this topic I have not found any discussion of this question.

- Could asking God to show us His will be the wrong question? Could it be similar to the Jews awaiting the coming of the Messiah? The Israelites had been waiting and praying for a Messiah through more than 400 years of silence. Many were sincere and alert for His coming, but when He arrived He was not what they expected. The Son of God was right in front of them, but they didn't recognize Him and so rejected Him. Why? They were looking for something else; they were waiting for a king who would establish his kingdom and restore Israel to its former position of strength. This kept them from understanding Jesus was God's Son. Could it be that we are doing the same thing? Are we looking for something obvious and right in front of us, but somehow not seeing it? Could this be our effort to put God in a box—a box where He doesn't belong and where He will not stay? Are we praying, "Show us Your will," but all the while God is telling us, "Do My will"?

- You know God made you and loves you and promises to provide and take care of you. You seek His will but then become certain that you have missed it. What do you do if you conclude that you made the wrong decision?

Live with Assurance

The Path of Assurance suggests that the key first step in finding God's will is simply to delight yourself in Him. This allows you to live your life for His glory and enter the future with confidence. Paraphrasing Paul in Second Corinthians 4:16–18, *The Message* reads,

> *...Even though on the outside it often looks like things are falling apart on us, on the inside, where God is making new life, not a day goes by without his unfolding grace. These hard times are small potatoes compared to the coming good times, the lavish celebration prepared for us. There's far more here than meets the eye. The things we see now are here today, gone tomorrow. But the things we can't see now will last forever.*

Many people fail to take this important first step, as in this story about the life of Clarence Darrow.

John Herman, an attorney, had a lifelong ambition of meeting the brilliant criminal lawyer Clarence Darrow of the Scopes "monkey trial" fame. It was arranged for the two men to meet. Sitting in Darrow's living room, Herman asked him, "Now that you've come this far in life and you're not doing much lecturing or teaching or writing anymore, how would you sum up your life?" Without hesitation, Darrow walked over to a coffee table and picked up the Bible. This took Herman by surprise, since Darrow was an atheist who had spent much of his life publicly ridiculing Scripture. "This verse in the Bible describes my life." Darrow turned to Luke 5:5 and read from the King James Version: "We have toiled all the night, and have taken nothing." He then closed the Bible, put it back on the coffee table, and looked Herman straight in the face. "I have lived a life without purpose, without meaning, without direction. I don't know where I came from. And I don't know what I'm doing here. And worst of all, I don't know what's going to happen to me when I punch out of here."[9]

My hope is that as Christians none of us will be like Darrow, who waited until his life was nearly over before he realized that he had built it on the wrong foundation. Instead, *begin* your life with the *end* in mind, and don't miss this great truth! Delight

---

9 Account taken from Dr. Joseph M. Stowell, *Strength for the Journey* (Chicago: Moody Press, 2002), 130.

yourself in the Lord; devote your life to glorifying God and enjoying Him forever.[10]

Almighty Father and King of the Universe,
We come before You as broken people who are too often bound up in seeking delights that are far removed from Your will. We want to change and grow, but we are deluded into thinking that it would be too hard for us, that we could never be all that You want us to be. Cure us of this delusion, Lord. Help us to see that growing in You is a process we can start today, right now. We ask that You will increasingly take over our lives as we delight ourselves more and more fully in You. That may not be easy, but remind us that we can do all things through Christ, who strengthens us.
In the name of Jesus, amen.

---

10 The Westminster Shorter Catechism, Question #1.

Chapter Three

GOD GIVES YOU THE DESIRES OF YOUR HEART

God grants us not always what we ask so as to bestow something preferable.

—Augustine[1]

When our children were young, we purchased a new metal swing set with a slide, two swings, a teeter-totter and very bright paint. Everyone was very excited when I brought it home and removed it from its box to put it together. My dad was there to help me, and we started to follow the "easy to assemble" directions that were several pages long. After nearly two hours of work, our initial excitement had changed to boredom (for the kids) and frustration (for me and Dad). None of the parts seemed to fit together, and we weren't close to being finished.

We finally got the swing set together, and later that night I decided to take a final look at the instructions before throwing them away. "Surprise" would be a mild word to describe my feelings when I noticed an "important note" in bold print: "For

---

1 Augustine of Hippo Quotes. Goodreads, accessed September 25, 2023, https://www.goodreads.com/author/quotes/6819578.Augustine_of_Hippo?page=4.

your child's safety, all screws, nuts, and bolts must be checked and retightened monthly." There must have been more than a hundred of those little things holding the swing set together! The thought of taking the time every thirty days throughout the year to service them was mind-boggling.

That is the way it is with so many of our desires, isn't it? We buy things and think we own them, but in view of the time and effort required to properly maintain them, they usually end up "owning" us. For example, it's like buying a new car (which we then have to keep clean, change its oil and tires, register, insure and pay taxes on, etc.), not to mention a boat or new home!

Psalm 37:4b
The Desires of Your Heart

When you first read Psalm 37:4b, you might think it refers to those types of new things, since in our culture the "desires of our hearts" implies God will meet our immediate wants—whatever we want, and right now! But in this verse the term "heart" means the "center of the human spirit, from which springs emotions, thoughts, motivations, courage and action—the wellsprings of life."[2] So Psalm 37:4b should be understood to mean, "God will give you what you actually need." It does not say that God becomes a kind of genie in a bottle granting your wishes. Although that sounds great—like the prosperity gospel just for you—God has something much better in store.

Receiving the desires of your heart means that over time as you come to delight yourself more fully in God, He introduces new desires within you. These will be what you need the most, not something superficial or fleeting. Instead, He will meet you at your deepest need, beyond what you could think or imagine.

It is not a matter of getting what you want from God; that is not the meaning of His giving you "the desires of your heart." Rather, God will first change your desires; then He will instill within your heart the desire for the things He wants to see in you. He won't just give you something you think you need; He will change what

---

2 Note, Psalm 4:7, NIV Study Bible, 10th Anniversary Edition, Kenneth Barker, gen. ed. (Grand Rapids, Michigan: Zondervan, 1995), 783.

you think you need to match His desires for you. Then He will give you those new desires. You will no longer want what you previously thought you wanted. Now you will want what He desires for you. Those become the desires of your heart, and they bring true contentment.

Let me give you an example of how this might work. Imagine one of your co-workers seems to be the favorite of the boss. This co-worker has a gift of eloquence and a quick wit and, as a result, gets promoted quickly, even though he doesn't know much about operations. That is what you want, to be promoted and well compensated in your position in operations. You ask God for help, but your career seems to be stuck.

Instead of trying to figure out some way to get ahead, you recall the story of Onesimus and Philemon and begin to focus more and more on God, delighting in Him. You then get the idea that rather than being envious of your successful co-worker, you might be able to help him improve his operational skills. As you do this, his regard for you increases, and when he gets his next promotion to another department, to your surprise he asks you to go with him. Over time this results in your becoming the lead trainer for the company. God didn't immediately give you the promotion, but as you began to delight yourself in Him by serving others, God changed both your desire and the way it was fulfilled.

God will give you desires and dreams of what the future could hold—dreams of what you will do, of how you will live and serve. "I want to be an artist or an author, a teacher or a leader, a great spouse, a strong parent for my children, or...." Have you ever felt exhilaration about your future? Maybe at one time it seemed almost limitless, and you knew that you could be someone great or do something special. In the words of Scripture, you could live "a life Jesus will be proud of: bountiful in fruits from the soul, making Jesus Christ attractive to all, getting everyone involved in the glory and praise of God" (Philippians 1:10–11 MSG). But then what happened? Where did those dreams go?

Can you honestly say that Christ does "everything he wants to do in and through [you]?" (Philippians 1:19 MSG). Take responsibility "for doing the creative best you can with your own life" (Galatians 6:5 MSG). You don't need to "push your way to the front"; instead, serve others, and in serving them you find yourself in Christ (Philippians 2:3–4 MSG). You can "provide people with a glimpse of…the living God" as you "carry the light-giving Message into the night" (Philippians 2:15-16 MSG). This is what Paul meant in Second Corinthians 10:15–16 when he said, "Our hope is that, as your faith continues to grow, our sphere of activity among you will greatly expand, so that we can preach the gospel in the regions beyond you" (NIV). You can do this anywhere, anytime and while doing anything, as long as you keep your gaze upon Jesus,[3] follow His moral laws, and make Him first place in your life.

These dreams don't end with your youth. But as you become an adult and more established, it gets easier to ignore your dreams or move them to the back burner while you work on the more "urgent and important" things. Each time you do this, it gets easier to do it again. And if you do it long enough, your dreams may become so deeply buried that they can no longer be heard. God didn't create you to live life like that. Your responsibility is to dream big, opening your life to His power and majesty and glory, and to allow Him to use you fully as you live out your desire for His glory.

Your dreams won't die. They may change and grow over the years, but instead of their dying you will experience Christ's joy and fulfillment as He allows you to dream—and dream big—and as you take the necessary steps to fulfill your new desires. It is not a matter of bringing your dreams down, but of allowing God to lift you up toward His vantage point. As you experience life on this higher plane, you see others in a new light as you develop love and compassion for them. You no longer push the needy out of your mind, but rather you embrace them. You no longer live a small life running scared of what may be ahead; instead, your life will be lived to the full, always reaching out to others. Things don't get in your way, obstacles don't distract you, time doesn't

---

3 Helen Howarth Lemmel, "Turn Your Eyes upon Jesus" (1922).

limit you, and the future doesn't scare you. Instead, you live with purpose and hope as you strive to become all that you can be through Christ.

Sam's Story

The story of a good friend of mine, whom I'll call Sam[4], illustrates this point. Sam and I met in third grade, and we were in school together through twelfth grade. Then we went our separate ways. I hadn't seen or heard from him for almost fifty years. When we recently reconnected, Sam told me his story. He said he had become rebellious while in college, and during his first job in the military he ignored God and His Word. After his enlistment was complete, he began searching for his next job. That is when his dad suddenly died, and Sam's perspective on life began to change.

Sam wasn't selected for any of the positions he applied for, and though he wanted to get married he had no prospects. He felt like he was "near the end of his rope." But then he met and became friends with a Christian man. As their friendship grew, this man shared the gospel with Sam and led him to a saving faith in Jesus Christ. Sam became serious about growing in Christ, and the desires of his heart began to change.

He soon met a wonderful woman, got married and started a family. He also found a position as a college professor as his faith continued to grow. Sam became more and more active in his local church and led his children into a vibrant faith. Years later when he retired from his teaching job, he joined the staff at his church, where he served until recently. Now he continues to serve God in mission work and on the board of a new ministry for needy children. Sam said he was amazed at what God had allowed him to do and experience.

As God changed his desires, Sam experienced the beauty of a new and exciting life. God will change your desires, too, as you become devoted to delighting yourself in Him. When that happens, you find new desires welling up inside, and things will begin to fall into place as God then fulfills the desires of your heart.

---

4 My friend graciously gave me his permission to use his story here.

Don't Wait

Once you realize that God is changing the desires of your heart, don't wait for others to approve or consent to the change. Support from your family and friends may be helpful, but move on with or without it. If the desired change seems too big to jump into right away, perhaps due to family commitments, begin small and see what happens. The next step will become obvious; as you take a step, you see the next step. But you must begin to respond to God's new desires within you.

For example, perhaps you want to know how much money to give to the Lord's work. Initially you might be hesitant to give anything because you are concerned that there won't be enough remaining for your family. But as you grow in your walk with the Lord, you realize that the Bible says to be generous and share your treasure with those in need (Proverbs 11:24–25 NIV). Thereafter you decide to start giving as you delight in the truth of God's Word. You begin with a small amount and then realize two things: first, you still have enough to meet your needs; and second, your gifts to others have become a source of happiness. In other words, you will find more delight in opening your hand and giving away your material possessions than in clenching your fist to hold onto them. Over time you may decide to increase your giving even more.

As you delight in God's Word and His majesty, you inevitably become a different person. Second Corinthians 5:17 says, "Therefore, if anyone is in Christ, the new creation has come: The old has gone, the new is here!" (NIV) This was true for King Josiah, who was ruling Judah when Hilkiah found the Book of the Law (see 2 Kings 22:8–20; 2 Chronicles 34:8–21). Scholars believe what he found was a portion of the Book of Deuteronomy, which had been lost during the reign of wicked King Mannasseh. When he read it, King Josiah tore his clothes in grief because he had ignored God's directives. He undertook reforms, which included purging the temple of other gods. As he was exposed to the truth, God changed his heart to be aligned with His Word.

Sometimes this change will be sudden, like with Josiah or a new believer who suddenly realizes that he has been on the wrong track. At other times it may be more deliberate, as with an immature Christian who is growing in his faith. However it happens to you, your love for God will increase and you will see all things in a new light. As Psalm 138:8 says, "The Lord will fulfill his purpose for me; your steadfast love, O Lord, endures forever..." (NRSV).

Although it may seem simple to explain what Psalm 37:4 means, it is more difficult to apply on a day-to-day basis. Think about how difficult it must have been for Onesimus to go back to Philemon and his former life as a slave after he tasted freedom. Or consider how hard it would have been for King Josiah to institute widespread reforms throughout Judah. Change is always difficult, and this is no exception. But it can be done. No matter how prominent you are or how unimportant you might seem, begin to delight yourself in the Lord, and then wait to see what happens as God grants you the new desires of your heart.

Personal Experience (Part 2)

It was a beautiful spring day when my wife and I were on a walk through the neighborhood talking about the future. I was around forty-five years old, and up to this point in my life I had been content to be a lawyer. But the desires of my heart were changing as I considered how I could more fully serve the Lord during the second half of my life.[5] I vividly recall the moment when I first mentioned to Cheri that I might leave the practice of law and instead go to graduate school to study God's Word full time. I had nothing specific in mind and had not previously said anything to her about it. When I told her (or perhaps more accurately "sprang it on her"), I wasn't sure what to expect, but I hoped for the best.

What was her reaction? I thought Cheri was going to call the men from the asylum in their white coats to pick me up and take me away! She was shocked and told me that I must be going crazy. Cheri asked, "Why would you want to walk away from a job providing significant income and opportunity, leave our friends, and start over again? What would that mean for our family and future?" Those were good questions, and I realized I hadn't

---

5 Bob Burford, *Halftime: Moving from Success to Significance* (Grand Rapids, Michigan: Zondervan Publishing, 2015).

thought it through and probably had jumped too far ahead in what I was thinking. But I knew that my priorities were changing and that studying God's Word was becoming more important.

As I prayed about this change, I found opportunities to serve and grow in God's Word without switching careers or going back to school. I went on a weeklong trip with our teenage son to a Christian outdoor wilderness camp, attended Promise Keepers events, helped organize a weekly Bible study at work, read the Bible every day, and changed churches to one pastored by a good friend.

Over time, years really, things slowly began to happen. Our kids graduated from high school and started college, and my wife and I were coming together about what might happen next. In anticipation of a change, we sold our house, which was quite a big decision because we had lived there for fourteen years and had many fond memories, and moved to a smaller apartment downtown. I began looking for the right graduate school, but I had no concrete plans when that might happen. I felt the desires of my heart changing, a little at first, and then more and more. I found myself thinking less about the things I desired a few years earlier and instead began to desire something else.

It felt like I was living in a fairy tale when the banking company where I worked announced that it would be sold. The company had always bought smaller banks, but now it was our turn. Since I was its chief legal officer, I was in the middle of this process. It took time, was complex and could have been derailed along the way. But after several months of negotiations, working with big-time lawyers from New York, visiting bank regulators and attending seemingly endless board meetings, public filings and shareholder meetings, the sale was finally completed.

Each of the senior officers had agreements providing payments in the event that our positions were eliminated in an acquisition. Since there could only be one chief legal counsel in the surviving company, the purchaser's lawyer would continue in his position and my job would be eliminated. I could have moved to another city as a junior member of the legal department of our new owner, but instead I took the departure package. Some people might have felt apprehensive or helpless in this situation, but it seemed to be the time for me to return to school and study God's Word. Making that change was something I had dreamed about, and it seemed too good to be true!

I visited a number of excellent seminaries, but something was missing for me. Although they were intellectually challenging, I needed something more practical with a hands-on approach. While in the Air Force I had been stationed at a base about two hours south of Chicago and had made several trips into the city and come to love it. Moody Bible Institute (now Moody Theological Seminary) was located there, and we decided to visit. I sat in on two classes and thought the professors were great; their style was casual and practical, and the students were diverse and intense. In short, it was exactly what I had been looking for, and I knew it immediately. Going back to school after twenty-five years was a big step of faith for me, one bigger than I had taken before, but somehow it wasn't as intimidating.

When we got back home, I applied and was accepted, so we packed up our things and moved to an apartment in Chicago. Even though we were looking forward to doing this, Cheri and I both found it difficult. We downsized and gave away many things we had obtained over the years. We said goodbye to our church, our friends, the city we knew with its many memories, and to Cheri's position with the public schools. Although we didn't recognize it until later, we were also leaving all the things that often provide fulfillment: wealth, power, pleasure and reputation.

This change was challenging for both of us, but what we were leaving behind just didn't seem important compared to what we were hoping to receive, as Paul said in Philippians 3:7–11. In Chicago we lived only two blocks from the school, which was in a part of the city formerly known as "Hell's Kitchen," but more recently called the "Miracle Mile." The year was 2000, and it being my fiftieth year, it was truly a year of jubilee (see Leviticus 25:10).

Thanks to the money from the departure package, I was able to attend graduate school and not be worried about how to pay for it. It also enabled Cheri to take a job at Moody, which meant she could be a part of that experience. It gave her the opportunity to attend chapel with me and sit in on some of my classes. Our faith continued to grow, and I learned so much I thought my head would explode! It was the most fun I have ever had as a student.

I can only describe this process as God changing and then giving me new desires as I delighted in Him. It was a wonderful experience. Our life in Chicago at Moody was amazing, and I had the opportunity to study God's Word full time with no distractions. I just sat in class with a big grin on my face, glad to be doing exactly what I wanted at the perfect time in my life. It was far from what I would have desired even a few years earlier, but I found more joy and fulfillment than I ever thought possible. You can, too.

Friends' Experiences

Some of my friends have shared stories with me about how God changed and then gave them new desires. One said that he faced a difficult decision about caring for his parents near the end of their lives. At first it seemed to be an obligation, and as they became progressively less able to take care of themselves, there was the option of moving them to an assisted living facility. However, they had always expressed a strong desire to stay in their long-time home, and he developed a God-given desire to help them do that. It was very difficult to manage their needs, but he felt appreciated and honored by the opportunity to care for them. Providing care didn't become less difficult, but he began to think of it as an opportunity to show love to his parents, not as an obligation. He took care of them not because it was the right thing to do, but because he wanted to do it. This is an example of how God miraculously gave him new desires as he grew in Him.

Another friend shared his story about how he had grown up in a strong Christian home where he had been exposed to great pastors, including his father. At age ten he knelt by his bed to receive Jesus and grew up loving the Lord. Later he was challenged to attend a Christian college by a visiting pastor, and while there he met the lady who later became his wife. From then on, their lives have been devoted to serving the poor. He also was blessed to become a theology professor and is now in full-time, cross-cultural ministry. Throughout his life he has felt the convergence of God's will as various new opportunities have opened. And as the desires of his heart were fulfilled, he devoted his life to serving others and, through them, the Lord.

Such a change for you may happen gradually as you begin to feel a shift in what you want, and as you become aware of the new desires, God will provide a miraculous way to fulfill them. You will find new opportunities for fulfilling your new passion. They don't have to be big; they could include teaching a lesson in Sunday school, keeping the nursery during the Sunday service, helping distribute food to the needy, singing in the choir or participating in a Bible study. They don't have to be as dramatic as moving to a new city for school, but something will occur that will give your faith an opportunity to grow.

These experiences will fill you with a joy you could never have imagined, and you will know God is giving you the new desires of your heart. These will be better than your former desires or anything you might have hoped for! But that can't happen until you yield to God and His Lordship, delighting in Him. Once you do that, something exciting happens as you cease to worry about what the next step will be. You begin to make decisions freely, relying on your good judgment and common sense. In my case I wanted to use the second half of my life to serve God and others, become a better father and husband, and study God's Word.

As things began to change for me, they also changed for my wife and kids as we grew together in the Lord. Thus by the time I went to Moody, I was truly living my dream. And it was so much better than anything I could have imagined would ever happen! This will happen to you, too, as you delight yourself in the Lord and thereby find the true desires of your heart.

Heavenly Father,
Thank You that You can change us through Your Word to become all You have told us we can be. As we bring our broken lives to You, we acknowledge that we are sinners saved by Your grace. We ask You to show us what it

means to delight ourselves in You as we grow in progressive sanctification. We know that You have given each of us gifts and abilities allowing us to serve You more fully as we become like Jesus. We ask that You radically change the desires of our hearts, from seeking more of what we want to trusting You to provide us with something far better. As we give up our insistence on protecting what we have, please give us what we need, for we know that only what You provide will truly satisfy the desires of our hearts.

In Jesus' name, amen.

Chapter Four

ALL THINGS WORK TOGETHER FOR GOOD

I have come that they may have life, and that they may have it more abundantly.

—John 10:10b (NKJV)

S noopy, the dog owned by Charlie Brown in the "Peanuts" cartoon strip, sat droopy-eyed at the entrance to his dog-house. He lamented, "Yesterday I was a dog. Today I'm a dog. Tomorrow I'll probably still be a dog. SIGH. There is so little hope for advancement."[1]

Perhaps we all feel like Snoopy sometimes: frustrated and with little hope. Sin keeps us living like a dog and sleeping in the doghouse. The good news of the gospel is that God, through His good and perfect gift of salvation through Christ, has made possible our release from the bondage of sin in our lives. That gift, freely given to us through Christ, gives us confidence in the abundant life promised.

---

1 *You're a Good Man, Charlie Brown,* the original 1967 off-Broadway production based on characters created by Charles M. Schultz. Music and lyrics by Clark Gesner.

Romans 8:28–29
Everything Works for Good

We have seen that the Path of Assurance begins as you delight yourself in the Lord and then find that your desires are changing to match His. This allows you to live in the wonderful joy that the Lord provides. But what happens next? The answer is found in one of the most beloved passages in all Scripture, which says:

> *And we know that for those who love God all things work together for good, for those who are called according to his purpose. For those whom he foreknew he also predestined to be conformed to the image of his Son...* (Romans 8:28–29 ESV).[2]

This is the final step in the Path of Assurance, and it begins with the assurance for those who love God that all things will work together for good. We might like to stop reading there because it seems to say that once you are a Christian everything will go well. It sounds like a sort of cocky optimism, doesn't it? But then the questions start. "Why are there wars?" "Why do bad things happen to God's people?" "Why doesn't God stop suffering?" The answer to those questions is found in the next verse; it says that things are not working together for our happiness, or good fortune, or the removal of evil from the world (yet). Instead, all things are working together for the good of conforming each of us to the likeness of Jesus. That puts an entirely different light on the promise of Romans 8:28–29. It means all things will work together for good as we become more like Christ.

Remember that Jesus was fully God and fully man, but unlike you and me, He was without sin (see Hebrews 4:15). It is easier to focus more on His holiness (being like God) than on His humanity (being like us). But since He experienced life in its fullness, He was tempted by sin, was misunderstood, arrested, persecuted and humiliated. Finally, He was crucified and buried. Jesus lived in a fallen world and part of His life was suffering. God wants

---

2 Some other verses are, "The Lord has worked everything for his own ends..." (Proverbs 16:4 NET) and "God is great—everything works together for good for his servant" (Psalm 35:27b MSG).

to conform you to the likeness of Christ, which cannot happen unless you, too, experience suffering. Hebrews 5:8 makes this clear: "Though he [Jesus] was God's Son, he learned trusting-obedience by what he suffered, just as we do" (MSG).

You undoubtedly hope for a pleasant life in a nice home with ample clothing, food and warmth. But living in a fallen world, you know difficulties will be a part of your earthly existence (see 1 Peter 4:12–13 NIV). So there will be times of illness, sorrow and death in addition to times of joy, celebration and happiness. But when your life ends, you will be resurrected and live forever in paradise with the Lord, which is the ultimate goal of every Christian. In John 6:40 Jesus says, "For my Father's will is that everyone who looks to the Son and believes in him shall have eternal life, and I will raise them up at the last day" (NIV). All things, good and bad, will then be seen to have worked together to conform you to the image of Christ (see also Romans 5:3–5 NIV).

As you focus on the immensity of God's love, don't become so concerned with the less important things that you miss what is really important. Don't focus on the path immediately ahead; instead, lift your eyes to see the glory of God. Praise Him, bring honor to Him, love and trust Him and abide in Him forever. As Ron Hutchcraft has said, "Walking in faith you can be sure that God will work the details of your life into something wonderful, and as you relinquish control you allow God to do what only he can do. After all, you don't need to be concerned with the plan so long as you know the planner."[3] At the end of your life when you look back, you won't focus on the difficulties you have faced. Instead, you will see a beautiful tapestry God has created through your life with all things working together for your good and His glory.

Romans 8:28–29 means that all things in this life, not just some things or occasional things, will work together for your good while conforming you to the image of Jesus Christ, in both your joys and sufferings. This is why what may seem to be a setback is actually molding you into the image of Jesus. Paul faced this dilemma when he was imprisoned. He had a choice

---

3 Ron Hutchcraft Ministries, Inc., *2021 Calendar – February* (Harrison, Arizona, 2020).

to either sit idly by while awaiting release or to make productive use of that time. That is when he wrote letters to the churches he had started. And as he wrote those letters, the Church throughout the ages has been blessed by his teaching. Similarly, the difficulties and illnesses you face are not what they seem. If you understand them as Romans 8:28–29 teach, you can find a silver lining in every situation. Paul says, "Each of you must take responsibility for doing the creative best you can with your own life" (Galatians 6:5 MSG).

Several years ago my wife became depressed after having a necessary surgery. Afterward she seemed unhappy and lethargic, and her generally sunny disposition was fading. However, with Christian counseling, support from friends and family, and reading the Bible and other helpful books, she began to recover. It was then she realized that with the Lord's help she could use her painful experience for the benefit of others. She let her difficulty bring her toward God, and so she decided to volunteer in the newborn clinic at our hospital. She worked there two afternoons and evenings a week after finishing her school job and was able to talk with women in difficult circumstances.

Cheri started coming home with a smile as she told me about some of her great experiences helping others going through tough times. Her cheery outlook returned as she allowed her difficulty to become a way to bless others, but first she had to make a conscious decision to see the silver lining in a difficult experience.

It was amazing to see how Cheri's surgery then impacted me years later. I had increasing pain in my hip for several years, but I delayed getting it X-rayed because I didn't want to consider surgery. Instead, I went to physical therapy, but as the pain intensified I finally went to an orthopedic doctor. He took one look at my X-ray and told me I couldn't wait any longer, so I scheduled a hip replacement.

While in the hospital recovering, I talked with one of the nurses about how busy she seemed to be, and I asked, "Is there anything I might be able to do to help out?" The nurse told me, "We need volunteers who have time to visit and talk with patients about their pending surgery." I listened politely and told her that

I would think about it, but I doubted I would ever voluntarily return to the hospital.

When we got home I mentioned it to Cheri, who thought it was a marvelous idea, and she suggested we could volunteer together as a team. That would be the first time we worked together, and we weren't sure how it would go. But we volunteered at the hospital until we moved away two years later, and it was wonderful. Cheri was a blessing as her smile cheered patients, and she also made friends with other volunteers. I encouraged patients by telling them of my favorable experience, which was rewarding.

But then I got to do something I liked even more. The hospital used a golf cart to transport patients from the parking garage to their appointments and needed another driver. I got the job. That was great because I don't play golf, but I finally got my chance to drive a cart. As I drove, I talked with patients, reassuring them that it was a great hospital and that they would get good care. Although there had been pain and difficulty before my operation, it was wonderful to help others afterwards. We could not have possibly foreseen the good resulting from Cheri's surgery years before, but as we trusted God, He worked it all into something that blessed others.

You, too, will see God's promise being fulfilled as your life unfolds. Don't believe things happen by chance, but trust God to work all things for good. You don't have to do great things, only what lies before you. The challenge is to glorify God when no one is looking, when you are not in the spotlight. Don't be discouraged by setbacks or illnesses that come your way. Instead, think about how God can use those difficulties to bring glory to Himself. Your obstacles will then become blessings, and as you move forward you will see God bringing events together into a beautiful pattern through the life you freely choose to live.

As John Wooden said, "Things turn out best for the people who make the best of the way things turn out."[4] Don't miss what God is doing! "Sometimes things have to fall apart before they can fall together. We may have to lose good things so that we can get

---

4 John Wooden, as told to Jack Tobin, *They Call Me Coach* (New York: Bantam Books, 1973), 71.

better things.["5] William Carey, the father of modern missions, put it simply like this: "Expect great things from God."[6]

Why This Can Be Difficult

Believing all things work together for good can be difficult because we tend to evaluate life by the outcomes we experience. For example, if you are admitted to the college of your choice and then do well there, most likely you would be convinced that you made the right choice. The same goes for your job choice, or your decision about where to live, etc. It is easy to believe, if things go well after a decision is made, that you have acted in accordance with God's will and that God is blessing your choice. Conversely, if things don't seem to be working out, you think it is because you made the wrong choice.

But what if that is not the case at all?

Consider this issue from another perspective. What if instead of having to make the "right" choice, you were free to make any choice? You could make all decisions without fear that you could make the "wrong" choice. Imagine you are a recent college graduate making a decision about your first job. You have two offers and must choose either working on the staff of a large church or serving as a missionary. You make a decision to become a missionary and you work hard, learn a lot and are successful as it leads you to other opportunities. Based on that, you are convinced that you followed God's will and are therefore being blessed. But consider what would have happened if you had instead become a member of the staff of the large church. You would have worked hard, learned a lot and become successful, which would have led to other opportunities. And if that happened, wouldn't you feel that God had blessed you because you followed His will?

It seems right for you to judge a situation by its outcome because a favorable outcome must mean you have followed God's will. But what if God does not consider the outcome at all, and instead

---

5 Robert Petterson, *The Book of Amazing Stories: 90 Devotions on Seeing God's Hand in Unlikely Places*, Day 77 (Carol Stream, Illinois: Tyndale House Publishers, Inc., 2017).
6 William Carey originally said this in his sermon to the Baptist Association meeting at the Friar Lane Baptist Chapel in Nottingham, England, May 30, 1792.

causes all things to work together for good? What if God is pleased with either choice? Then you would be in His will regardless. A good fictional example of this can be seen in the writing of Chris Fabry. While trying to decide whether or not to go down a long slide at a pool, one of his characters says,

> Then I looked down at my dad and he was waving at me and putting a thumb in the air, and his dad was standing up and had his arms hanging over the fence watching me. I half wondered if this is the way God is. Some think you have to go down the slide in order to please him. But maybe he's just standing at the fence smiling and reaching out for you.[7]

It is hard to look at things this way because it seems counterintuitive. As humans with limited minds, it is almost impossible to look beyond the immediate results to see what might have happened with a different decision. In other words, you are limited in your vision and cannot appreciate the complexity and beauty of God's ability to work any decision into something good.

Remember, your responsibility is to delight yourself in Him—trusting in the resurrection of His Son for salvation and living your life for God's glory. Then God gives you the freedom to make whatever decision you think is best, and He will work it into His plan for good and the ultimate triumph of His kingdom. This is a blessing too wonderful for words. It provides you with freedom from worry about whether a decision is God's will. It is so magnificent it is hard to grasp, which is why it is easier to judge events by their outcomes.

You Cannot Miss God's Plan for Your Life

It breaks my heart when I read books about God's will that refer to God's "Plan A." Those teach that you can miss Plan A and then be forever relegated to living out some lesser plan. This second plan may be a good plan, but it is not God's Plan A.

---

7 Chris Fabry, *June Bug* (Carol Stream, Illinois: Tyndale House Publishers, 2009), 276.

Where does this thinking come from? How can there be a plan for your life that is less than what God desires? Since God is all-powerful, how can "all things work together for good" not mean "*all things*"? Can you make a wrong decision that throws you onto a Plan B? Worse yet, what if you mess the next decision up, too, and then are forced on to the next lower Plan C? Imagine this happening over and over as one wrong decision leads to the next lower plan and so on. It would be hard not to simply give up by the time you reached Plan Y.

But the good news is that this cannot happen. As a child of God delighting yourself in Him and enjoying the desires of your heart, then all things, that is to say *all things*, will work together for good. There is only one plan for your life, and it is the one you are now living. It is not the plan you are looking for, or waiting for, or seeking a sign to find. No, it is simply the life you are living right now.

In another of his books, Fabry uses the fictional words of one of his characters to state,

> The truth is this: you don't need your circumstances to change in order to give praise to God. In fact, the best place to live the Christian life and participate with God in the plan he has for you is right where you are. So whatever task he has for you to do, whatever job you have, or if you're just out looking for a job, I don't care what it is, God wants to work through you today, right where you are.[8]

The good news is that you can't miss God's plan for your life. You can only live it, experience it and enjoy it as you revel in the wonder of His love and kindness.

To understand this more fully, think about some situation in your life. Maybe it is your job or where you are living. Then think about how things would be different now if something else had happened earlier. For example, I think about Cheri, my wife

---

8 Chris Fabry, *Almost Heaven* (Carol Stream, Illinois: Tyndale House Publishers, 2010), 217.

of fifty years, who I met while I was at the Air Force Academy in Colorado, the state where Cheri had been born and had always lived. I was almost not admitted to that school because my grandfather had diabetes. There are medical requirements for admission to the service academies, and, as a result, I had to take a glucose tolerance test to see if I, too, had a tendency for diabetes. The first time I took the test it was inconclusive and the doctor reviewing my results could have disqualified me.

If that had happened, I would have never left West Virginia and would not have met Cheri. Then of course we would not have gotten married, and we would have each lived out completely different lives. Either life would have been within the will of God, and we will never know what might have happened. It doesn't matter. All we can know is what actually happened and keep moving forward. But would something like that have put us on a Plan B? No, because with God there is no Plan B! This is because God works all things (meaning *all things*) for good for those who love Him.

I was talking with someone who is convinced that God had a Plan A for her that she should have followed. The plan was that after graduating from college she should have focused exclusively on God's Word and preached the gospel as an unmarried missionary in Europe. But since she didn't realize that when she graduated, she instead got married and became a teacher, thereby inadvertently missing her Plan A. Although she and her husband have been happily married for years, she believes she has been off track and on Plan B ever since she failed to become a missionary.

That thinking goes like this: God loves you and has a wonderful plan for your life. Once you accept Christ, you must immediately step into God's single best plan for your life or you will forever be on a lesser plan. After being reduced to living Plan B, if you make yet another mistake, you fall onto Plan C, and so on. But would God have a plan that includes a path downgraded by your mistakes? What if you are frequently wrong in discerning God's will about where you should live, what you should drive, or what you should do? What if your spouse also misses her Plan

A, and it pulls you both further off track? And what if she wasn't supposed to be your spouse in the first place? If you are hoping to figure out God's will for all of this, what chance would you ever have of staying on Plan A? If this were my view of finding God's will, I would constantly be looking back trying to figure out what I had done wrong.

That is impossible, isn't it? Yet how many people live a life of regret about what might have been if they had only done something else? Of course, there are times when you might feel frustrated and discouraged, thinking you are in the wrong job or living in the wrong city, but that doesn't mean you have missed God's will for your life. God's will is more basic and fundamental than that. It simply requires you to trust God and not worry about missing the so-called "Plan A."

Jesus taught this when He met a person known as the rich young ruler. The man asked how to have eternal life, and Jesus told him to obey God's commandments. When the young man said he was already doing those things, Jesus said, "…sell your possessions and give to the poor, and you will have treasure in heaven. Then come, follow me" (Matthew 19:21 NIV). The young man left discouraged because he was rich. (Read the whole story in Matthew 19:16–22.) The focus is usually on the fact that the man loved being rich, but notice what Jesus did not say. He did not tell the man to sell all his possessions and become a priest, gardener, tax collector, vineyard owner, cook, soldier or anything else. Why? That is not a critical part of God's plan. Instead, God's will for that man (and for you and me) was to live a life following Jesus and giving glory to God.

Another example comes to us in the story in Luke 8:26–39 (NIV) of the man with demons who lived among the tombs in the region of Gerasenes. What is significant here is what Jesus said to the man after the demons left him and went into a herd of nearby pigs. The man asked to go on with Jesus as a disciple, but Jesus told him, "No, return to your home, and declare how much God has done for you." He did not tell the man to go home and train for evangelism, or become a shopkeeper, or study to be a teacher; in fact, He did not suggest any sort of profession at all. He simply told him to go home and tell others what had happened to him. The man could have had a great job, a menial job or no job at all. Yet if his specific job had been a part of God's plan, wouldn't Jesus have said something about it?[9]

Why then do we conclude that God's plan for our lives must include those details? God isn't concerned with what we do as long as it brings glory to Him. You must keep moving ahead to see what God has in store for you. You can be confident that God is working things for good in your life right now. God's wonderful plan for you is to live your life for Him, regardless of what else you do. In other words, God wants you to live your life glorifying Him, and, if you want, to also be a baker or a banker or anything else you choose![10]

Jesus taught that after you believe His Word, you must "hold it fast in an honest and good heart, and bear fruit with patience" (Luke 8:15 ESV). In other words, your career could be anything and you could live anywhere; you could be married or not, have kids or not, or be rich or poor. You could be doing anything in any field, but with saving faith and patience, you will bear much fruit. How can this happen? It happens because God makes sure it does. He gives you the desires of your heart and then works all things in your life together for good as you are conformed to the image of Christ.

Imagine a person who has a saving faith but who is having difficulty due to sickness, or raising children, or at work, etc. The person must be patient, trusting God to work things for good in his life and allowing him to bear fruit. You must be confident that God will do the same for you while waiting patiently to see the results.

Rather than living on pins and needles hoping to correctly fig- ure out Plan A, God expects you to move on with life and trust Him to work things out. You can be confident as you think things over, weigh the pros and cons, and then make the decision that

---

9 There are other examples of Jesus giving instructions for future behavior, and none of them include directions about the specific career a person should choose in his or her life.

10 In an episode of "The Chosen" television series, we are told that "everyone has a much larger job than just their trade" ("The Chosen," Season 1, Episode 3, "Jesus Loves the Little Children," television series, directed by Dallas Jenkins [2019]).

seems to make the most sense. You don't have to wait for a sign from God but can keep moving forward into the life that is coming. It may not be obvious immediately, but over time you will see that good things come from your decisions. The same conclusion applies to all other decisions you make in life: God is faithful and can be trusted.

So don't feel intimidated if a big decision is in your future. It is not there to frighten you, but to allow you the freedom to choose. As you exercise your ability to choose, you gain confidence for when the next decision comes. You may still feel like you are standing on the edge of a cliff, but you are more comfortable than the last time you were there. The cliff may not seem so high, and the fact that things worked out the last time will help you take another step of faith. Remember, God provides a lamp for your next step (Psalm 119:105), not headlights for the entire road ahead. God will work all things together for good as you freely take the steps that you believe, in your good judgment, will allow you to be your best.

Soar Like an Eagle
While walking in our neighborhood I have seen large birds flying elegantly overhead, but for some reason smaller birds attack them. Being more maneuverable and faster, the little birds gang up on the big birds and attack mercilessly, forcing them to flee. The majestic soaring of the bigger birds is beautiful, but it provides no defense against the rapid-fire harassment of the smaller birds.

God's desire for you is to mount up on wings as eagles—to fly high and live your life for Him (see Isaiah 40:31). You are meant to soar, to ride the currents of God's love and grace in freedom. But do you ever let your fears and worry about the future limit you? Could those simply be the "smaller birds" forcing you to give up your desire to soar? Ask yourself, "Do I have confidence that God will work all things for good so I can avoid being grounded by the need to know the entire flight plan before I take off?"

God doesn't want you to live in uncertainty or confusion. The Path of Assurance allows you to live your life to glorify Him, wherever you are and whatever you do.

Dear God,

It is indeed a marvelous thing to know You are working all things together for our good. Although we can't conceive how You can accomplish this, we thank You for it. It is far bigger, bolder and better than anything we can imagine. You are a great God who sees the end at the beginning. Your ways and thoughts are far above ours. Let us trust that everything will work together for good as You conform us to the image of Your Son.

We love You, Lord, and acknowledge that You want us to live as Your children and be part of Your kingdom. We thank You for both the good times, which we enjoy, along with the difficult times, which we would like to avoid. We know that even in our suffering You are making us more like Jesus. We pray that Jesus, who lived, suffered, died and rose from the grave, will always be our role model.

We thank You for all of our situations—sickness and health, happiness and grief—because our lives are in Your hands. And as we consider the end of our lives here on earth, we know that we will be raised to eternal life with You.

In the precious name of Jesus, amen.

Chapter Five

QUESTIONS (PART 1)

*Give thanks in every situation because this is God's will
for you in Christ Jesus.*

—1 Thessalonians 5:18 (CEB)

Having introduced the basics of the Path of Assurance,
let's take a look at how it would apply to some "real life"
situations. The following questions and answers will help
you see how to do that.

Question 1: Where is God in times of illnesses?
Answer: For many of us, especially as we age, dealing with illness
becomes a primary concern. It could be our illness or that of a
spouse, a child or a friend. The thing that frequently concerns
us is whether the illness might be terminal. All of us know that
we will eventually die, and we expect it, but at the same time we
aren't thinking it will happen now. We think, "Maybe when I'm
older, but not right now. There are still so many things I want to
do. I will be okay if it happens then, but certainly not now." Or we
might think, "Why me? After all, I'm a Christian. Doesn't God
love me and care about me?"

In 2010 just after we arrived in South Carolina, I went to the
drugstore to get a flu shot. Having been in the Air Force, I had

been required to do this for years, so when I retired I continued to get the shot, not thinking much about it. But about ten days after I got this one, I noticed a tingling in my fingers and then in my toes. At the time I was painting our bathroom and attributed the tingling to that. But it continued and became more noticeable, gradually spreading fully into my hands and feet.

Having just moved, we didn't have a doctor, so I had to quickly locate one. He thought my symptoms were the result of stress and ordered blood tests, telling me to come back when he got the results. I began to feel like I was wearing long, tight gloves and boots as the tingling continued to spread into my legs and arms. The doctor had a couple of ideas about causes, but because he wasn't sure he referred me to a neurologist whom I saw two days later.

By the time I got to his office, my legs were losing coordination, and I stumbled up the two stairs to his office. I was definitely concerned. The neurologist was a Russian doctor who had a noticeable accent. "Merrell, I vant you to go to zee hospital," he said after a five-minute examination. I asked, "You mean for more tests?" But he said, "No, you have a very rare condition"— impacting about one person in a million, called Guillain-Barré syndrome (GBS). "If you don't get to the hospital before zee tingling reaches your lungs or heart, you vill die."

"What did he say?" I asked myself. "Did he say die? Did he say that to motivate me to get to the hospital quickly, or could it be true? He said I had something serious, but what did he say the name of it was?" I rushed home, got some things together, and called my wife at school. We were at the hospital within the hour for further testing.

In one of those tests I was lying on my back on a flat table in my hospital gown with my wife and the neurologist in the room. He attached some electrodes to my legs and told me not to move while he ran the test. Then I felt what I thought must have been 1,000 volts of electricity jolting through my leg, which immediately flopped off of the table. The doctor, with his strong accent, said, "Merrell, vould you plez hold your leg steel." I thought, "Are you kidding? How can I possibly hold my leg still?"

It is hard to believe, but, while lying there, I was reminded of my training at the Air Force Academy during which our cadet "captors" talked with Russian accents while questioning us in a mock prisoner-of-war experience. Now, while lying on the hospital table, I could almost hear the doctor saying, "Tell me, comrade, where is zee enemy base." Cheri and I still laugh about it to this day, but, believe me, it was no laughing matter then.

Eventually I was able to hold my leg still, and the doctor confirmed that I had GBS. I was admitted to the hospital and confined to bed for five days of in-patient treatment. Guillain-Barré syndrome is a rapid-onset muscle weakness caused by the immune system damaging the peripheral nervous system. Mine was caused by my recent flu shot that had been designed to respond to an expected outbreak of the swine flu. That shot caused a reaction in which my body's immune system attacked my nerves.

After five days I was discharged from the hospital and sent home, but I was feeling very weak. Several weeks of therapy followed, and it took a year for me to fully recover. I am very fortunate to have had a neurologist who was able to diagnose GBS quickly. Many United States doctors see this disease so rarely that it can take much longer to diagnose, and the nerve damage can become permanent. But my neurologist had practiced in Russia where GBS is more common.

I can definitely relate to the fear of being permanently disabled or of being about to die. When illness comes, as it probably will, and you are faced with the fear of dying, being disabled or losing your mind, what should you do? Do not underplay the concern that is natural, but remember that God is in control and working all things for good while conforming you to the image of Christ. And that necessarily includes suffering.

When it happens, your responsibility is to force yourself to look for the silver lining in your situation. Perhaps it is to make you more compassionate and caring. Perhaps it is to slow you down so you can take time to appreciate the blessings all around you. Perhaps it is to cause you to consider whether there is something you should do to improve your health and fitness. Perhaps it is to change your perspective on life, allowing you to see where your

51

priorities should be. Or perhaps it is something altogether different. The key is for you to realize and appreciate that something good will come out of the situation and to glorify God in it. As you seek God, He will help you deal with and deliver you from your fears because love drives out fear (see 1 John 4:18). It isn't easy to do this and it doesn't come naturally, but as you grow in your faith, it is possible.

You have probably known people faced with an early death and have seen how they react. Although some people are mad and fearful, others are at peace. The key is to see the silver lining in what has happened from God's point of view. As you do, you will recognize that the spirit of the Lord is within you. Guillian-Barré Syndrome encouraged me to become more compassionate and caring toward others, particularly those who have a serious illness.

When illness comes, you must be confident that it will work for good—to conform you to Christ—knowing even death will bring with it your ultimate victory. You will find there are ways to use your experience to bring good to others. But whatever you do, don't allow the illness to become a source of resentment or bitterness toward the Lord, who is working all things for your good. Be comforted by Psalm 34:4, which says, "I sought the Lord, and he answered me; he delivered me from all my fears" (NIV).

Question 2: What are we to do when facing an important decision, such as whether to get the Covid vaccine?
Answer: After I had GBS, I was told not to get any more vaccinations because any new vaccination could trigger a recurrence of GBS. I had been very fortunate to fully recover because about thirty percent of people who have GBS experience ongoing disabilities or death. In any event, I didn't want to take a chance of getting GBS again. On the other hand, Covid is also a terrible disease, with hospitalization, prolonged recovery or death all possible.

I had a wide range of emotions about this issue and was confused, thinking first I should get the Covid shot and then being sure I shouldn't. Most of the time, though, I couldn't make up my mind about what to do. Of course, I continued to read the Bible and pray, and I talked with my friends, especially those who are doctors, and with others. I sought God's wisdom, but I felt the pain of indecision and uncertainty.

I would have liked to be able to ask God how things would turn out with and without the shot. I couldn't sleep at night and often found myself preoccupied with this question throughout the day. I asked my doctors every question I could think of that might help. There was peer pressure to get the vaccination for the good of the community, which somewhat balanced the fear of getting GBS again. But, at the end of the day, I just didn't know what I should do!

It is not God's will that I should make the wrong choice. He desires that I flourish. I can live my life for Him regardless of what I decide about the Covid shot. This is not a matter of God's will. God's will for me is to live as a follower of Jesus by putting my faith and trust in Him. As I do, I am given the freedom and responsibility to make choices using my best judgment each day. Sometimes I won't know if I made the best choice, but still I must make a decision and move on.

James 1:5 says, "If any of you lacks wisdom, you should ask God, who gives generously to all without finding fault, and it will be given to you" (NIV). It was not a matter of finding God's will, but of finding His wisdom. So instead of trying to find God's will, I prayed for wisdom. As I did this, I got closer to deciding what to do about the shot, realizing I might still come to the wrong conclusion. I also realized that if I made the wrong decision and ended up in the hospital or paralyzed or in some other condition, I would still have the opportunity to live for God and share my faith with others.

It is easy to put God in a box when we ask Him to show us His plan for our lives. We limit Him to the confines of our immediate problem. His plan is not as small as we might imagine. God's will is not about what sort of soup we should be eating, or what car we should be driving, or whether to get the Covid vaccination. He has a much bigger goal in mind, and so should we. It isn't about us at all, but about His kingdom, growing in His likeness and spreading the good news.

We are saved through Him and are given the opportunity to serve Him wherever we are and whatever we are doing. So don't be so caught up in "the details" of your life. Keep your eyes focused on the big picture. As Ron Hutchcraft says, "When we own the reality of the bigger plan of God, we begin to see beyond our situation to our assignment as an ambassador for Christ."[1] That is God's plan, and through His blessing and grace it can become yours!

Question 3: If you have two good opportunities and must make a choice between them, how do you know what to do?
Answer: We had a contract for the sale of our house in Colorado and were planning to move to a new home in Pawleys Island, South Carolina. But then something happened that forced us to reconsider. A few days before it would be time to leave, the telephone rang....

The year was 2010, and we had been living in Colorado Springs for six years. I worked at a large Christian ministry, and as usual my wife had a great job in the nearby school system. If you have not been to Colorado Springs, you are missing something. The entire town, with a population of about 500,000, sits in the shadow of Pikes Peak, which is more than 14,000 feet tall and dominates the entire western skyline. The summers there are wonderful, and the Rocky Mountains are beautiful throughout the year. However, during the long winter, anyone who has been there for more than a few years (there aren't many true natives) will tell you that Colorado enjoys a "dry cold" that feels warmer than places suffering through a "wet cold." Sadly, I couldn't distinguish the difference and was usually just plain cold.

Cheri's family lived only sixty miles away, so it was a great location. But while we were there, her parents' health rapidly declined and, after brief illnesses, both died within eighteen months of each other. It was a very sad and difficult time, but it was more bearable for us because we were living close enough to visit and provide assistance when needed. Both of her parents

---

1 Ron Hutchcraft Ministries, Inc., *2021 Calendar – August* (Harrison, Arizona, 2020).

had been wonderful people who were warm, friendly and loving, and we miss them very much.

While we were still in Colorado Springs, I had an idea that I might become a mediator. Things were going well with my work with the ministry, but I was considering what might come next. I wanted something based in the law that would require less rigorous work. I learned that to become a mediator required only one week of training, so I traveled to Pepperdine University in Malibu, California, for the class. It was a great course and I enjoyed both the area and the academic work. I graduated and received my certificate as a mediator.

I then created a brochure describing my services, chartered a corporation and obtained a website for my new company, called Business Resolutions. I hoped it would be a great way to help people who might otherwise end up in litigation, which is generally a very bad decision for everyone except the lawyers. I also investigated some local mediation opportunities but found nothing was available. I tried to get business using contacts I had made around the country. I got one small job and a couple of volunteer opportunities, but after several months there had still been no significant work. That is when we decided to move to South Carolina, hoping to find work there and be closer to our kids.

When the telephone rang that day in 2010, it was the supervisor of mediation services for the city of Colorado Springs, one of the many places I had sent my brochure to but had heard nothing. The lady calling told me there was an open position and asked if I could come in for an interview. I wondered, "How could this be? For months I had been looking for just such a position, and now when we are ready to leave, I get a call?" In the rush of emotions and in more than a little frustration I thought, "What should we do?" I didn't have a job lined up in South Carolina, but that was not unusual. Should we stay or should we go? Suddenly there were two good choices in front of us.

Do you ever find yourself in a situation with two great opportunities? Could one of them be the position God intends? If it is, how can you be sure you pick the right one? Could you really follow the Path of Assurance and choose whichever one you think is best, using your best judgment, and move on with your life?

What did we do? My wife and I talked about our options, one of which was to remain in our comfortable lives in Colorado near her brothers and I would work as a mediator. If we did that, Cheri could keep her job. Or we could move closer to our kids and my family in West Virginia and hope to find another job. Cheri had proved that she was almost instantly employable, but not me. Why had the phone call come when it did? Did it mean we should stay in Colorado? We thought the situation through, using our God-given abilities and common sense. We prayed for good judgment and God's blessing. We realized we were already so far into the moving process that we really couldn't easily change our minds without serious consequences. We concluded that it would be best to make the move.

Did we have second thoughts about our decision? Of course we did. In many ways it would have been easier to stay in Colorado. We will never know what might have happened if we had stayed, and we certainly didn't know then what would happen when we moved. But despite the uncertainties we decided to move to South Carolina and were confident that we had God's blessing either way.

When you are in a similar situation, the Path of Assurance lets you make a logical decision based on your best judgment and move ahead. This is not to suggest that God doesn't care what you do; He does. He wants you to make God-honoring decisions and take God-honoring actions. Then He can work whatever specific choice you make into good while you are conformed to the image of His Son. God is so great, you don't need to worry about what will happen next.

Heavenly Father,
   So often we ask that You show us Your will when we need to ask instead for Your wisdom. Teach us to ask You for the wisdom we need, and then trust that You will provide it. Trust is such a delicate thing. Help us to place our trust, all of our trust, in You alone.

We know that You are the source of all our blessings. Let us see that at times we must endure difficulties so that You can build the character of Christ more fully in us. Fill us with patience and always keep us from hesitation and doubt.

For we ask this in Jesus' name, amen.

Chapter Six

THE TIME OF YOUR LIFE

*God can do anything, you know—far more than you could
ever imagine or guess or request in your wildest dreams!*
—Ephesians 3:20 (MSG)

Delighting yourself in God makes it possible to trust Him more and more. But it is impossible to know what will happen as God first changes and then gives you the desires of your heart. God promises that He will bring about good while you become more like Christ. When that happens, the results will be bigger, bolder and better than anything you might expect. You will be amazed at how God will use you.

Why Are You Using a Typewriter?
For years we have known a Christian couple in Indiana. Our friend, Pete[1], spent his career working as a systems engineer for a company that designs, manufactures and sells large machinery. Almost thirty years ago Pete and his wife, Phyllis, decided to donate some clothes to a nearby crisis pregnancy center. The center was then operating in a small space rented from a local Catholic church and had no full-time employees. While waiting for a receipt after dropping off the clothes,

---

1 Pete has generously given me permission to use their names and story here.

Pete noticed that the receipt was being typed using a typewriter, so he asked, "Why are you using a typewriter and not a computer?" The manager told him, "Because we can't afford to buy a computer." Pete had already built one for his personal use, and he said to the manager, "If I gave you a computer, would you use it?" She replied, "Yes, we would." Pete then built and donated a computer—his first gift of a computer to a ministry.

Pete would never forget that when Phyllis first became pregnant, she had delivered a healthy baby boy but, shortly thereafter, was diagnosed with a deadly brain tumor at the same hospital where she had the baby. The doctors told her that if they had known she had cancer while pregnant, they would have recommended that she have an abortion because of the likelihood that her cancer was hereditary.[2] Pete knew that they would never have agreed to an abortion, and he wondered if that could have been the reason they had decided to donate the clothes to a pregnancy center.

Fast forward to today: the crisis pregnancy center has grown and now has a building of its own and several full-time paid staff, including nurses. Pete has donated dozens of updated custom computers to the pro-life center over the years, which provides ultrasound photos to women considering abortion. When they see the images of their baby, they frequently decide to give birth. Pete also now donates computers to other ministries around the world, including some in Africa.

More than sixty million babies were aborted after the Supreme Court's decision in *Roe v. Wade* in 1973, so you might wonder how many lives have been saved by Pete's gifts. Of course, no one knows. When Pete first went into the clinic, all he planned to do was donate clothes, but he had a heart seeking to serve, and God used him in a powerful way. It is only after the passage of time that something seemingly unimportant, like donated clothes and a computer, can be seen as transformed by the Lord into something that brings glory to His kingdom. Pete remarried after Phyllis died, and his wife, Barb, now calls this "Pete's computer

---

2 Through many answered prayers and miracles, Phyllis outlived her projected three- to six-month life expectancy by sixteen years. Sadly, Phyllis lost her battle with cancer, but before she died, she saw her son standing at the foot of her bed in his high school graduation cap and gown. Although Phyllis had been unable to communicate for more than a year, she was able to raise her hand as tears streamed down her face in thanks for seeing her son on his graduation day.

ministry." Pete told me, "Now that I'm retired, I realize this is my way of using the skills God has given me to bless others."

Recently when Pete's three-year-old dishwasher broke down, he purchased a replacement. Then he realized that the cause of the problem with the original dishwasher was easy to fix. After he repaired it, Barb said she preferred to use their original dishwasher, so Pete moved the replacement out and put the original back in. This left them with a new dishwasher they didn't need. The next day while delivering computers to a local ministry, Pete noticed the ministry needed a dishwasher to replace their old one, so Pete donated his extra dishwasher and helped install it. Could this be the start of "Pete's appliance ministry"? He doesn't know, but he remains alert to watching for ways he can serve.

This story shows how God will take your desire to serve Him and bring about results that you never thought possible.

The Life of Joseph

In Genesis 37–50 is the story of Joseph, who was one of the twelve sons of Jacob. As a young man he was sold by his jealous brothers and taken to Egypt. During the next thirteen years Joseph lived as a slave, and then he was imprisoned for a crime he did not commit. He could not foresee anything good coming from his suffering, but he continued to live a life devoted to God. Then his life suddenly changed when he interpreted a dream for Pharaoh about a coming famine. Overnight Joseph was released from prison and promoted to the second most powerful position in Egypt, with the task of preparing for the famine. Later his family came to Egypt needing food, and his brothers were afraid Joseph might be vengeful. Instead, he told his brothers, "It was not you who sent me here, but God..." and "...you meant evil against me, but God meant it for good..." (Genesis 45:8; 50:20 ESV). God used the difficult experiences of Joseph's life to bring him to a position of power that ultimately saved his people.

Joseph could not have foreseen the wonderful things that would happen for the benefit of the entire Israelite nation. Similarly, God will take the difficult and painful experiences in your life and work them together into something you could have never imagined.

Things may not happen in the way you expected, but when you look back you will see that God has worked them together into the time of your life.

Personal Experience (Part 3)
I was the oldest student in our class and, at age fifty, older than all but two of our professors at Moody. For the first few weeks I probably looked strange sitting in class smiling, just happy to be there. Each class was packed with information I was excited to learn, and each assignment presented challenges I couldn't wait to tackle. The professors seemed interested in what was going on in our lives, and we were invited to their homes for meetings and meals. I could not imagine how things could get any better, but I was about to see that the best was yet to come.

During spring semester of 2002, there was a meeting about the school's summer mission trip. As a lawyer I had always felt I was too busy to go on mission trips, and as we sat in the auditorium I was excited about the possibility of my first trip. At the same time I was wondering if I should leave the few available spots to younger students. When it was announced that the trip would be to Cameroon and Kenya, Africa, I immediately got cold feet. I really didn't have any desire to go there, so I asked the professor in charge of the trip about it, hoping he would discourage me. Instead, to my surprise, he said, "You are exactly who we want on this trip."

I didn't know anything about Africa except what I had seen years before in Tarzan movies. After our meeting I received a book from a friend listing the top ten things that can kill you in Africa, and number one was a hippo attack! This simply reinforced my misperceptions, and then I learned about yellow fever, malaria, tetanus and other health issues. Despite these concerns I signed up, attended pre-trip meetings and was designated the trip photographer. Finally we boarded a plane for the long flight to London (about eight hours), a layover there (about four hours), and a final flight to Nairobi, Kenya (about ten hours).

Upon arrival we cleared customs and late that night entered a crowded and very hot airport filled with unusual sounds and smells. There was a crush of people in the airport offering various services, like getting us something to drink or providing directions. We finally got into our van and were taken to a missionary guest house where the guys were all assigned to a big room filled with beds, each with a mosquito net. Those nets have a very fine screen and are hung from above the bed. You pull them over your body at night to protect yourself from mosquito bites and thereby prevent malaria. They work; that is, they work unless a mosquito gets under the net while you're crawling into bed! But I am happy to report no one got malaria and there were no hippo attacks. That was a relief.

We had a team of eighteen students on the trip, including a Moody student from each of the two countries we would visit. The student from Kenya was Martin Simiyu; I didn't yet know him but over the years we would become close friends. Very soon I realized that Africa was filled with rich natural resources and friendly people who didn't ever seem to be in a hurry. There was also good, if different, food and bottled soft drink products—we were warned not to drink water out of a tap. At first Nairobi looked like a modern city with cars and people everywhere, but as we traveled there and into the villages, we saw a very different situation.

Here are a few photos that provide a feel of what we experienced while we were there.

Our first stop was Kibera, a slum in Nairobi, which then had a population estimated to be over 500,000, all living in unimaginable poverty. This is the largest of ten slums in Nairobi.

While everyone else was inside an AIDS clinic in Kibera, I walked around the compound and saw a young boy sitting by himself. The colors and patterns on his sweater were beautiful, and the lighting seemed to make his face fade into the background. He looked as though he was a shadow who might hardly be noticed amid the pain in the clinic. Since he didn't speak English, I never found out if he or a relative had AIDS. For me this photo captures the very deep pain sometimes found in Africa.

This photo captures the quiet beauty of the people of Africa. It shows a young woman preparing food and selling vegetables as she operated a small market. She was selling exactly the same thing as the vendors in nearby booths. Despite her challenges, the joyful look on her face was apparent. Martin told me that although the people in the slums didn't make much money, it was more than they could earn in their village. So while paying very little to their landlord for a place to live, they were able to send some money home to their family each month.

This photo reminds me of the depth of the poverty in much of Africa. It is of a young girl who I first thought was playing grown-up and wearing adult shoes. But then I noticed that the shoes were worn out and had high heels that are not user-friendly on the muddy roads. I learned that she was wearing shoes she found in a trash pile. They were her only shoes, and, although they were too big for her, wearing them was better than going barefoot like many of her friends.

This photo shows the vast gap between the rich and poor in Africa. Kibera slum is located near the home of the President of Kenya, on whose grounds there is a beautiful golf course. Here is a young boy looking at the golf course from behind the fence in the slum, scratching his head while wondering what was going on. I, too, wondered how to reconcile the very rich playing golf in view of the unimaginable poverty nearby.

While in Kenya I also visited a child who Cheri and I had sponsored for several years through a large ministry. His home was in a village not far from Nairobi, but riding with an employee of the ministry over the pothole-filled, dirt road seemed to make it a long trip. We pulled off the road and walked on a foot path the last mile to his family compound where he lived with his parents and brothers. Everything I saw there was unbelievable; there was no plumbing or water, no electricity or lighting. They lived in mud huts, and everything was very primitive. The mother showed me how she made bread cakes on a stone, and the father showed me how he took care of the family's large garden using a sharp stick. No one in the family spoke English, so the ministry employee had to interpret everything. It was a surreal experience.

I had taken gifts for the family, including bags of sugar and flour and bars of soap, but I didn't know it was also the custom for them to give something to a visitor. The mother was embarrassed because she didn't have anything for me—not that I wanted anything. Then she disappeared into her hut and came back with a beautifully woven large bag that she gave to me. As I took it, I wondered what on earth I would do with it. It wasn't until I got back to the United States that I realized it had been her sewing bag, since I found a spool of black thread inside. The bag, with the thread still inside it, now hangs in my study. This story always brings tears to my eyes as I think about her generosity in the face of such dire poverty. Here is a photo of that moment:

We met dozens of other Africans while there, including one woman who was approaching a hundred years old and had never met a white person until we arrived for a visit. These people all asked the same thing. They wanted to know if God had forgotten them and how they could overcome the difficulties in their lives.

All of us on the trip began to think about what we could do to make a difference. Kenya is a very big country with many tribal groups, each with its own language and customs. Africa is three times as large as the continental United States. Our fundamental goal was very straightforward: we wanted to help the people we met. But how? You will read about the answer to that question in Chapter Seven, and it again demonstrates that God works things together in a majestic, beautiful and intricate way as we trust in Him.

> Heavenly Father,
> We often see pain and suffering while living in this fallen world. We know that there are kids playing in mud-filled streets without shoes all around the world, scratching their heads while watching the rich play golf nearby and silently wondering, "Why?" We really do want to help, but we don't know what we can do. And there is so much suffering that we wonder if what we could do would really make a difference anyway.
> We ask that right now You would increase our confidence that our prayers do make a difference and that as we continue to serve You as Joseph did, You will allow us to comprehend how much our small gifts can accomplish. We therefore dedicate our five loaves and two fish to Your kingdom. We bring our gifts with open hands and hearts, trusting that You will multiply and use them in unforeseen ways for Your glory.
> In Jesus name, amen.

Chapter Seven

AND GOD DOES THE IMPOSSIBLE

With man this is impossible, but with God all things are possible.

—Matthew 19:26 (ESV)

A s part of my Air Force training, I participated in a mock prisoner-of-war exercise high in the Rocky Mountains. During that time we were held in a "prison camp" where we were forced to do manual labor during the heat of the day. At that altitude (approximately 8,500 feet) the sun's rays were particularly intense, and it was a bright, sunny day. In addition, Colorado is a very dry state, and we were there during the very driest part of summer. As part of our orientation we were warned that no matter what, we should never drink the water from the many beaver ponds that dotted the mountains. This was because that water was laced with all sorts of microbes and health-threatening bacteria that could make us very sick. Then, to make our training more realistic, we "prisoners" were not given any water during that long, hot day.

As time drug on, I began to experience thirst in a way I never had before or since. Of course, I had been thirsty before, but not like that day. My lips became parched and actually cracked, and my throat got so dry that it became sore. It was painful and agonizing, and soon all I could think about was water. While wandering around gathering wood for my captors, I walked through an area that on other days would have been considered a muddy spot in the path. It had a very small trickle of water running out of a nearby beaver pond. But on that day I was so desperate for anything to drink that I reached down, acting like I was picking up wood to avoid detection. Instead, I scooped up in my hand some brownish, foul-smelling water.

Heedless of its possible adverse effects, I rapidly drank as much as I could without attracting attention. Putrid as it was, I can still remember many years later how wonderful it was to have something to drink and how much it eased the pain in my body and my intense cravings. I was surprised that I risked drinking water that could have been contaminated. But I was more surprised at how overwhelming and painful the experience of literally drying up was and how badly I craved the water my body desperately needed.

That taught me what people who live in deep poverty routinely experience. All of us have seen pictures of poverty in Third World countries. We have seen children with hunger in their eyes, meat hanging in the open air for sale in the markets covered with flies, and the dusty dirt roads without cars—only people walking. On one of my trips to Africa I noticed that there was no trash can in my room and asked about it. I was told, "Here we don't throw anything away." Millions of people know what lasting hunger and thirst are and how hard it is to survive while desperately needing so much.

While on that first trip to Kenya, my first inclination was to just give them something—anything, really—that might ease their pain. For example, on that trip I was with three boys admiring the chicken coop they had built at the orphanage where they lived. I asked if they named their chickens. They said, "No. We eat them." Then one of the boys noticed that I had a few pencils in my backpack and asked me for one. They were grinning as they thanked me for giving them each a pencil and also for the chewing gum and paper I had with me. I wanted to give them more, but I hadn't thought to bring anything else. All of us on that first trip experienced the feeling that we needed to do more—an urge to find a way to help overcome the needs we couldn't help but see. The following is the story of what happened after our mission trip to Africa in 2002.

A Fateful Meeting

For our classmate, Martin Simiyu, life was never easy. His life began in a small village in western Kenya, Africa, where he and his family lived in deep poverty. Despite the many challenges he faced, he always had a dream for a better future. He did well in school and eventually made his way to the United States to attend Moody Bible Institute, where we were both students. Knowing all too well about the problems back in Africa, Martin decided to become a mission major, and he helped organize our trip to Kenya.

It was near the end of that trip when Martin and I had a fateful meeting. I was sitting alone outside our guest house when Martin joined me. We began to talk about what we had seen, and our conversation then turned to what we could do to change things. Martin had been thinking about this for some time and had talked to several others on the trip. He told me that he knew we could make a difference in the lives of the people there. I told him we could not just go back and do nothing, thinking that it had been an interesting trip but that things couldn't be changed for the better. Martin said he would like to begin a ministry that would change peoples' lives in the villages, and I responded, "Well, let's go in and tell the others." We did, and our group discussed it and prayed for God's guidance and wisdom. But at that point actually doing anything lasting seemed impossible.

After our return to Chicago, there were more prayers and meetings until finally the idea of a new ministry began to take shape. Conversations continued, and after several months action began. This new ministry was chartered, a board elected and meetings held. After getting a second master's degree, Martin returned to Africa, and the work began. Looking back at the formation of the ministry, it is clear that God was using

Martin, me and others. We all joined together at just the right time and place to begin a ministry called Possibilities Africa. It has continued for almost twenty years, has grown and now blesses many people throughout Africa.

Once we got the ministry started, it was time for the next big step: finding a way to fund our work. I cannot explain how difficult this can be. We had a great idea for ministry, a plan of execution, the start of a record of success, and an honest leader in Africa who wasn't in it for the money. But still, we had almost no money. We had some graduate school students who weren't rich and had only a few contacts. And when I first contacted people about the ministry, they weren't very interested. Some thought that Africa was hopeless while others had obligations and interests that kept them from giving to a startup ministry. I have since learned that startup ministries and new restaurants both have about the same chance of making it, with only about thirty percent surviving after ten years.

We didn't see how we could raise enough money. Then one of the people Martin had met while getting his second master's degree became interested and started giving, and a few others followed. These gifts enabled Martin to leave his church position in Nairobi and undertake full-time work for the new ministry. He told me that without those few donations he would have probably ended up like so many others who come to the United States for an education. Despite having a desire to make a difference, they return home only to find that their urgent need for money keeps them from getting a chance to develop their dreams. If that had happened to Martin, it would have left him with no time to start Possibilities Africa, and our story would have ended before it began.

We continued to reach out to others with news of our ministry, using brochures, photos, newsletters, a video and other means. I talked with friends living in Virginia, and they agreed to host a get-together in their home while Martin was back from Africa. We drove six hours to their house to find that of the twenty people expected, we had an audience of only five people. Martin gave a presentation, but at the end of the evening the only donation we received was from our hosts. It was a relatively modest gift, but it was most appreciated.

And then something wonderful happened. My friends kept giving a small amount each month. But a small amount given regularly adds up, and over the years they have become one of our larger donors. Since then many others have given, and the ministry has grown and grown. It has been said that if you can explain what happened, then it can't be God at work. There is no way anyone associated with this ministry could ever explain how this happened. We have a website, *https://usa.possibilitiesafrica. org*, and seventeen full-time employees in Africa, and we serve in seven countries with plans to keep growing until the entire continent is reached.[1]

Many people have helped with the ministry, some mentioned by name in this chapter, as well as countless others, who have brought their passions, interests and abilities to create a beautiful tapestry for God's kingdom.

Key People
Doctor John ("Doc") Fuder
Doc Fuder was one of the professors who led our mission trip that summer. An excellent teacher and Godly man, he taught, motivated and inspired students and was one of the favorite professors at Moody. Before the mission trip, he organized and led several critical early-morning prayer meetings, and he kept us alert to see what God was doing while we were in Africa. When we got back, he was a part of the meetings that eventually led to the creation of Possibilities Africa and was one of its original board members. Doc played a key role in keeping enthusiasm high and things moving along, and he always had an upbeat and positive attitude about our hopes and dreams for Africa. He and his wife, Nel, hosted meetings in their home and were essential to the start of the ministry. Now on our advisory board, Doc is a sounding board for

---

1 For more information about the ministry of Possibilities Africa, see Rachael Varnum's article, "With God All Things Are Possible," in the Winter 2023 edition of *Moody Alumni & Friends* magazine, available at https://www.moody.edu/alumni/connect/news/2023/with-god-all-things-are-possible/.

new concepts and has returned to Africa several times as he continues to serve with the ministry.

Matt Shada

A student from Moody who played a key role in the startup of Possibilities Africa was our class president, Matt Shada. He talked with Martin about the needs in Africa, and he wanted to make a difference. As we approached graduation Matt had a number of opportunities to join large Christian ministries. Not sure what he should do, he eventually met with a small group of people from his home state of Nebraska about starting a new church there. The position felt right, and he and his wife moved to Omaha and started Steadfast Bible Fellowship. Matt and I got to know each other better as members of the Board of Directors of Possibilities Africa. Matt organized the first mission trip from the United States to visit Possibilities Africa in Kenya. Several of his church members saw the work of the ministry firsthand, were moved by what they saw, and have been diligent in supporting our work and sharing the story ever since.

Doug Shada

Matt's dad, Doug Shada, was a pastor in central Nebraska who heard about Possibilities Africa from Matt. Doug was charming and persuasive, and he led a large established church. One of the first methods Possibilities Africa used in its ministry was similar to the Heifer Project International, where a cow is sold to a family at a reduced price to provide milk. That family must be trained to take care of the cow and must donate its first calf back to the ministry so it can be sold to another family. We prepared a publicity video featuring the story of the cows and the impact they had on the lives of people who received them. Unknown to us when we made the video, a number of Doug's church members were cattle farmers. When they saw the video, they were touched, and funding for Possibilities Africa began to take off. Doug served as chairman of our board, and before he died of cancer he led several mission groups to Africa as Possibilities Africa continued to grow.

Doug Reed
Through 2019 our volunteer board had been handling activities in the United States, but as we grew it became apparent that we needed a full-time person in America to coordinate work with Martin in Africa. We let a few people know, and Doug Reed, a pastor at a church in a small town in Nebraska, applied for the job. Years earlier when Doug was in college, he volunteered with Campus Crusade, showing the Jesus video in Africa. He had been assigned to work in Tanzania, but at the last minute was reassigned to Kenya. While there he saw the poverty and other needs, and he was convinced that the key to change was with the pastors. So when we offered him the position, we all knew it would be a perfect fit. In the past three years with Doug's leadership, Possibilities Africa has grown rapidly and now has a budget approaching one million dollars, which is amazing.

How Possibilities Africa Works
The philosophy of Possibilities Africa is virtually unique. Most of the ministries in Africa are led by the people from the sponsoring country, usually Westerners. This generally means that, one, the ministries provide what Westerners think the people of Africa need, and two, the ministries place Africans in the position of believing they must say "yes" when asked if they want what the sponsoring group provides.[2] When Possibilities Africa started, we did not do that, primarily because those of us from the United States had no idea what the people in Africa needed. So we relied upon Martin, who knew what was needed and how it should be provided.

Possibilities Africa works through pastors in each village as they come together and agree on their most pressing need. But instead of providing it for them, Possibilities Africa tells them it is their responsibility to do something about it. In other words, Possibilities Africa doesn't give handouts to the people of Africa, and this has an amazing effect. It frees the people from dependence upon Western decision-making and instead allows

---

2 Steve Corbett & Brian Fikkert, *When Helping Hurts: How to Alleviate Poverty Without Hurting the Poor...and Yourself* (Chicago, Illinois: Moody Publishers, 2009).

them the freedom to make the choice about what to do themselves. As a ministry we train the local pastors, and then they take the message to their congregations. This leadership training is critical because once the message is implemented in one life, it spreads to another, and another, until the entire village becomes involved.

You might wonder, "Why have the billions of dollars in gifts and aid poured into Africa had so little lasting result?" The answer is simple. It is because Africans do not realize they have the capacity to make decisions without dependence on outsiders to make choices for them. So, Africans simply wait to receive their next handout. Most mission agencies and their programs usually cause the African people to rely on others. But once Africans realize they can rely on themselves, they quickly understand that another handout won't solve their problems. And with that their situation begins to change. This is what Possibilities Africa has done, and it works! Each of those who supported the ministry got the opportunity to do their part as Martin followed God's leading step by step. There was no thunder and lightning, but as we took a step, we then saw the next.

A diverse group of people joined the ministry at different times, at just the right time. Was there any way to predict that a small group of graduate students could start a successful international ministry? Could anyone have known what God would do when desires were placed before Him by people delighting themselves in Him? Would anyone have been able to think about something so big and far-reaching? Yet since God works all things together for good, why should we be surprised? Why should we ever have doubts or fears?

During the time Possibilities Africa was getting started, none of us sat around wondering if this was God's will. We didn't seek a sign or look for a shooting star. We wanted to serve God, we had a big dream and a small team, but we believed things would work out for good. This could only have happened with God's blessing, and it shows God can and does work all things into something much bigger and better than anything you could imagine.

The motto of Possibilities Africa is, "With God, all things are possible" (Matthew 19:26). I have seen that it is true, and, believe me, it is wonderful to behold! You can count on your heavenly Father to work all things for good as you serve Him.

Reflect God's Love
Several years ago I was staying at a hotel in Colorado Springs and the window in my room provided me with a perfect view of Pikes Peak to the west. That is the mountain that inspired Katharine Lee Bates to write a poem that became the song "America the Beautiful," and when you see it you quickly realize it really does have "purple mountain majesties." The afternoon I arrived, the sun was going down behind the mountain, and it was dark and imposing.

Early the next morning as the sun was beginning to rise across the flat plain lying to the east, I was surprised to see a very small but bright spot of light shining out of the darkness on the side of the mountain. It began as a pinpoint of light, but gradually it grew in size and intensity until it became so brilliant I could no longer look directly at it. At first I wasn't sure what it was, but later I found out a cabin had been built years ago on the side of the mountain. I was seeing the sun reflected by one of its windowpanes. Even though the window was old, broken and dirty, the sun shining on it produced a dazzling brilliance. It had been invisible the night before, but now an ordinary pane of glass could suddenly be seen from miles away. Its radiance was not due to any energy or source of power it had; rather, it was in the right place to simply reflect the sun's incredible light.

Whenever I feel discouraged, I think back to that experience. I know that I don't need to rely on any wisdom or power of my own. Instead, I only need to allow myself to be used by God to reflect a small part of His brilliant love and light. In Second Corinthians 3:18 we read, "we can be mirrors that brightly reflect the glory of the Lord. And as the Spirit of the Lord works within us, we become more and more like him and reflect his glory even more" (NLT).

Live to reflect the glory of God and experience the time of your life as you watch God do the impossible!

Father,

We praise You for who You are and what You do through our lives. We thank You for allowing us to have a part in building Your kingdom and to have the time of our lives as You do the impossible. We thank You for giving us a wide open and spacious life we can enjoy. You are a loving Father who wants us to live abundantly during our time on earth and who doesn't hide Your will. We thank You that it is open before us, and we ask that You keep our eyes fixed on You as we move always forward into the wonderful life You provide.

In the name of Jesus, amen.

Chapter Eight

THE BETTER WAY:
THE PATH OF ASSURANCE

Led by a new paradigm, [we]...see new and different things...

—Thomas S. Kuhn[1]

book written by Thomas S. Kuhn in 1962 introduced an important new concept. He called it a paradigm shift, which he defined as a major change in how people think that upends and replaces a prior widely held belief. For example, the change in peoples' belief that the earth was at the center of the universe (the Ptolemaic system) to the belief that the sun lies at the center of the solar system (Copernican system) was a paradigm shift. Similarly, the shift from believing the earth was flat to the belief that it was round was another.

That is what this book, *It's Not Complicated*, is about: it suggests a fundamental change in how to see God's will that is simpler, clearer and more effective than what has been proposed in the past. It is called the Path of Assurance, and with it you

---

1 Thomas S. Kuhn, *The Structure of Scientific Revolutions* (Chicago, Illinois: University of Chicago Press, 1970), 111.

begin to realize the usual questions about God's will, like what you should study or where you should live, are not so important. Those are the first things most people consider as part of God's will, but they are more correctly seen as the details of your life. God will work those details into His plans for good, regardless of which decision you make. The Path of Assurance seems so simple that some will criticize it for that reason. To them I ask, "Is it any simpler than the method for our salvation?"

To be sure you understand this concept, let's start by considering the basic principles that underlie our Christian faith.

- **The Bible is God's message to you.** How can you know that? Consider a text with sixty-six books, written by approximately forty authors over a period of more than 1,500 years. How could such a book be internally consistent, telling one single story from start to finish? How could the Old Testament prophets have foreseen events that would not happen for hundreds of years? Why has it been a source of faith, hope and comfort to so many, and how did it become the bestselling book of all time? Why has it generated faith through the ages? None of this is an accident. The Bible is the message from God, inspired by the Holy Spirit. You can trust it as true.
- **The Bible explains that God created the earth and everything in it.** It says, "The heavens declare the glory of God; and the firmament shows His handiwork" (Psalm 19:1 NKJV). Think about the order and beauty of His creation. As you stand at the beach watching the sunrise, you cannot help but praise God for His bounty and the wonder of life. At a mountain retreat you see the majesty of the world and the entire universe. When you travel you learn about the diversity and complexity of life and what you have in common with others around the world. At home you love and appreciate your family and shelter, warmth and food. All of these point to an all-powerful, good and gracious God.

- **The Bible teaches you to appreciate the mysteries of the galaxy.** For example, why do you feel like you are sitting still in your living room when actually you are flying through space as the earth spins, orbits the sun and moves through space with our galaxy? Do you realize that it would take 1,300,000,000 earths to fit inside our relatively small sun? Or that to travel across the Milky Way at the speed of light would take 100,000 years, and that the Hubble telescope has already discovered over 15,000 similar galaxies?

- On the other hand, think about the nature of things so small that they can be seen only through powerful microscopes: that you have about thirty-seven trillion cells in your body; that your heart beats about 100,000 times each day; and that your eyes can distinguish seven and a half million colors.[2] Finally, think about the chances that you are alive among the eight billion people on earth today. These blessings are far too complex to have happened naturally or by accident. If you simply accept the obvious, you must conclude that God created it all and give Him thanks.

- **Finally, the Bible tells us that at just the right time, God became incarnate and lived among us as Jesus,** who was born about 2,000 years ago. With His birth God provided a path open to everyone, everywhere, to know Him. It is estimated that more than eighty percent of people in the world believe in some sort of higher power. Of all the gods worshiped by religions around the world, Christianity is the only one in which people can experience the full extent of the love their Creator has for them. As you put your faith in Him and trust in His death and resurrection alone for salvation, you are known as a believer.

Believers want to know the will of God for their lives, but it is easy to become confused and eventually to abandon the search.

---

2 Chris Stefanick and Paul McCusker, *The Search* (Greenwood Village, Colorado: Augustine Institute, 2020), 21, 24. See also Guillermo Gonzalez and Jay W. Richards, *The Privileged Planet* (Washington, DC: Regnery Gateway, 2004).

The Path of Assurance provides a new method to find and follow His will. As Paul wrote in Philippians 3:12b, "I press on to take hold of that for which Christ Jesus took hold of me" (NIV). This method can be summarized as follows:

1. First, delight yourself in the Lord, trusting in Him alone—this is your prime responsibility, and it is a big one. Delighting in God includes reading His Word, obeying His moral laws, praying, being in fellowship with others, meditating on God's goodness and loving others. When you do this, you will inevitably find your delight in Him.

2. God then changes your desires to align with His, and He will provide those new desires for you. This is a process, not an overnight event. Begin wherever you are spiritually and grow in progressive sanctification as you become a new and different person. As Second Corinthians 5:17 says, "Therefore, if anyone is in Christ, he is a new creation. The old has passed away; behold, the new has come" (ESV).

3. Next, God will cause all things—that is to say, everything in your life, both good and bad—to work together for good in making you more like His Son. This will lead you to do things you never dreamed of doing, provide opportunities you could never have imagined, do the impossible and fill your life with purpose and joy. God wants you to live and grow in resemblance of Him and, as His children, to trust in Him more and more.[3] He will bring others into your life who will work with you to create a beautiful tapestry, weaving them and all of their gifts and talents together to bring glory to the Lord.

4. But right now we live in a fallen world marred by sin and evil. God allows pain, suffering and death, but that was never His desire. His creation was to be perfect, but because of sin, humankind must now be reconciled to God.

---

3 Ephesians 1:5a says, "God destined us to be his adopted children through Jesus Christ because of his love" (CEB). See also Keith Carroll, *Created to Relate* (Newburg, Pennsylvania, Relate To God Press, 2016).

So whether you are a poet or professor, an astronaut or administrator; whether you live in Nebraska, New York or Nevada, or a suburb or a slum—it doesn't matter. Those and similar aspects of your life are not crucial to God's plan. God's will for your life is much more basic and fundamental and important than that. A line from a recent television series puts it this way: "Everyone has a much larger job than just their trade."[4] God's will is the same for each of us; it is perfect; it will complete you and give you peace. It provides endless energy and boundless strength, and it is immense, glorious and extravagant, beyond anything you could ever imagine or expect or request in your wildest dreams. You must keep your attention there.

You will find challenges and opportunities to do more than you ever imagined, and they will be the things you freely choose. God can use whatever you decide to do in your life as a part of His earthly kingdom. He will work that into good as you are conformed into the image of His Son, Jesus. You are free to live your life to the fullest—to explore and pursue alternatives, to follow your dreams and find the courage to live a life of adventure as you are more and more conformed to the image of Christ. When facing a decision, simply use your good judgment and common sense to make your choice.

Your eyes will be opened to opportunities for service, and you can freely choose what specifically you want to do, knowing that, ultimately, you will live eternally with God. That may happen after you have had a long life of ministry bringing many others to faith, or while you are married to a special person who loves and supports you. Or you may have been born with a significant medical problem the doctors cannot cure and impedes your abilities. Or you might die at an early age in an automobile accident, or at age thirty-five as a result of illness, or any number of other causes that don't include a long life followed by death at an old age.

Consider the story of Ahimelech, the high priest in First Samuel 21:1–9 and 22:6–23, living in Nob, known as the "city of priests." He was a Godly man who lived faithfully with eighty-five other

---

4 "The Chosen," Season 1, Episode 3, "Jesus Loves the Little Children," television series, directed by Dallas Jenkins (2019).

priests, all serving the Lord. David came to Nob and requested Ahimelech's assistance in feeding his men, but he did not tell the priest that he was running from King Saul. Ahimelech gave David consecrated bread from the altar and the sword David had used to kill Goliath. However, the priest's kindness was observed by one of the king's officials, who reported it back to Saul. When Saul learned of the meeting, he was incensed and sent for Ahimelech and the eighty-five priests of Nob. He accused them of giving aid to his enemy and, without a trial, sentenced them all to death. Then King Saul ordered the mass killing of all the "men, women, children, infants, and its cattle, donkeys and sheep" in Nob. While it is not surprising that we prefer to focus on the miraculous life of David, there is another part to this story. Could the death of the priests have been part of God's will for them—innocent people brutally murdered on orders of the king?

Like the senseless slaughter of the priests of Nob, many early Christians were also killed. "Some faced jeers and flogging, and even chains and imprisonment. They were put to death by stoning; they were sawed in two; they were killed by the sword. They went about in sheepskins and goatskins, destitute, persecuted and mistreated—the world was not worthy of them. They wandered in deserts and mountains, living in caves and in holes in the ground" (Hebrews 11:36–38 NIV). And today many are persecuted or killed indiscriminately in frequent wars and shootings.

Was that God's plan for their life? Does it mean God doesn't care about what happens? Rest assured, there is a much bigger picture; it is what God sees. Our lives here are not the end of our story. Due to our limited minds all we can understand is what happens here on earth. But there is more. A lot more! Our eternal life in heaven with the Lord will be without pain or tears—only joy and ultimate satisfaction. Can you imagine it? Can you see it? Do you believe it? You don't have to fear death. Instead, live your life in the freedom that comes from a loving God, confident in the future with Him.

This is more fully explained in Second Samuel 12:13–25. There David is confronted by the prophet Nathan for sins of adultery and murder committed against Uriah and his wife, Bathsheba.

David confessed his sin to the Lord, but in addition to other consequences, David was told that his baby boy would die as the result. David prayed, pleading with God that his child would not die. He also spent his nights lying in sackcloth and fasting. When the baby died seven days later, David got up, washed, changed clothes, worshipped God and ate. The Bible relates,

> *His attendants asked him, "Why are you acting this way? While the child was alive, you fasted and wept, but now that the child is dead, you get up and eat!" He answered, "While the child was still alive, I fasted and wept. I thought, 'Who knows? The LORD may be gracious to me and let the child live.' But now that he is dead, why should I go on fasting? Can I bring him back again? I will go to him, but he will not return to me"* (2 Samuel 12:21–23 NIV).

David is confident that he will see the child again, and this is often seen as the story of a man after God's heart. But think for a moment about this from the perspective of the baby. Ask yourself, "What was God's will for him? Why would he die after only seven days on earth?" How could this be, especially since God has told us in Deuteronomy 24:16 that children will no longer be responsible for the sins of their fathers? It is because death is not what your life here is all about. No, it is rather about salvation. There will be a life after death that will be wondrous, no matter at what age we die. This brings comfort when we think about people, especially young ones who lose their lives too early. Instead of living here, they are moving on to something better with God. God provides eternal life, and, as a result, we know death is not the end of our story.

Our understanding of God's plan is incomplete. God controls all of the alternatives, each depending upon what choice you make. All you need to know is that God wants you to trust Him. Then you can simply stand back and see how God will work everything for good as you are conformed to the image of Christ. This is part of an intricate plan that is beyond what we could ever comprehend. In that bigger plan all things work together for our individual good, and it will ultimately lead to the conclusion that God has planned for the world. That is the plan people sometimes refer to when they say, "God is working all things out in His own way and in His own time."

All of this is further complicated by the fact that God already knows the end result of these plans. He alone knows what is going to happen at each step along the way. So while you are totally free to make decisions on your own, God will work them together for your good as well as weave them into His plan for this world. That is where our understanding of this process ends, while the rest of it—the complex part, the part we all wish we could know and understand—must be left to the Lord. We then trust God, who made us and loves us, to bring all of this together. "We never really know enough until we recognize that God alone knows it all" (1 Corinthians 8:3 MSG).

Be Careful What You Ask For

Let me challenge you to consider the question of God's will from yet another perspective. What would happen if God had one, and only one, Plan A for your life?

Imagine you have a grandchild or nephew about fourteen years old. One day the child excitedly tells you what he wants to be when he grows up. "I am going to be an astronaut!" You are surprised to find that he already knows about the training required and understands basic astronautics. Getting caught up in his excitement, you begin to see some of his vision for the future. You tell him what you recall about John Glenn and the exhilaration you felt during the early space flights years ago. You also talk about Apollo 11 landing on the moon and Apollo 13 returning to earth despite serious damage.

But suddenly you remember the truth about your family. You stop and look directly at him as you say, "That would be an exciting and wonderful career, but I hate to tell you, you can't do it." At first the young child is silent as he considers this. Then, not really believing you are serious, he asks, "What do you mean?" You explain that while being an astronaut would be great, it's not possible because you already know God's will for his life. And that is not it. Instead, you tell him, "Like your father and grandfather before you, you must become a teacher. Of course, you can teach anything, anywhere, but you must be a teacher. Our family has always been teachers, and years ago God decided this was His will for our family. Our ancestors knew this, and we have always followed His will for our lives. So there isn't much else to say." The child chokes back tears and walks silently out of the room.

Could something like that really happen? It did happen. In the Old Testament Book of Numbers we read about the God-given roles for the descendants of Levi, who served as the priests. This occurred in about 1400 B.C., and there were several clans involved; but for now, consider the clan of Merari. Merari was one of the three sons of Levi and his clan had originally been charged with taking care of the crossbars, posts, bases and accessories of the tabernacle (Numbers 3:36). At that time there were 3,200 men in the Merarite clan (Numbers 4:44). God assigned their work to them and thus it was the will of God for their lives. "At the LORD's command through Moses, each was assigned his work and told what to carry" (Numbers 4:49 NIV).

Imagine a young boy of the clan of Merari who had a dream of doing something other than carrying the tent posts. Maybe it was singing, but it could have been any dream or desire. When he asked his parents about joining the choir, they had to say no because they knew that God's will for their family was to carry the equipment needed for the tent of the tabernacle. That was a great calling, but was it the calling in the heart of all of the young children of the clan?

The carrying of tent equipment for the tabernacle would be abandoned years later when the Israelites arrived in Jerusalem, where a temple would be built. You might ask, "Were the Merarites then free to choose their career?" That would make sense because after the temple was built there would be no need to transport parts of the tabernacle, but instead of disbanding them, King David assigned new roles to them. He said, "Since the LORD, the God of Israel, has granted rest to his people and has come to dwell in Jerusalem forever, the Levites no longer need to carry the tabernacle or any of the articles used in its service" (1 Chronicles 23:25–26 NIV). He then assigned to them other duties as caretakers for the temple of the Lord (1 Chronicles 23:28–31).

For hundreds of years the Merarites were doing exactly what God told them to do. They were following His will for their lives and could not make that decision for themselves. This story comes from the Old Testament, and the Israelites were the chosen people. God does not deal with us today as He did with the Israelites then, so that situation does not apply directly to us. But can you imagine if your parents insisted that you follow the choice they believed God had preselected for you? Could it feel like you were being forced into a mold that really didn't fit? What about the free and spacious life God promised?

Think about it like this: you now have the choice to live anywhere and do anything you want so long as it brings glory to the Lord. Why would you limit that freedom by insisting there is one and only one right answer for every decision you face? As a believer you may live life in any manner pleasing to God. This is marvelous and provides you with a life that is bigger, bolder and better than anything you could imagine. Ultimately, it leads to life forever with the Lord. What could be better?

Your problems and questions may be much more numerous and difficult than anything I have written about. My hope and prayer is that the Path of Assurance will provide you with the tools you need to bring about positive change. Bad things may happen to you, but when they do, don't give up or lose heart. God has made it easy for you to follow His will. Ultimately, at the end of your life, whenever that may be, having been conformed to the image of Christ, you will pass over to life eternal with the Lord! That will be the final miracle of your life.

Heavenly Father,
We know that when we place our faith in Jesus Christ, we will abide with You forever in our heavenly home. We thank You for providing this assurance. Help us see that what happens here on earth is being worked into the details of Your eternal plan. Let us experience energy

and strength as You work us into Your will for Your creation. We thank You for the free and open life that allows
us to use the judgment You have given us to choose what
to do next, without worry that we might make the wrong
choice. And we ask for wisdom to make decisions with
confidence and strength in You, our eternal hope.

We pray in Jesus' name, amen.

Chapter Nine

WHAT ABOUT MISTAKES?

Never allow the thought, "I am of no use where I am,"
because you certainly can be of no use where you are not.
—Oswald Chambers[1]

It was a temptation Mike[2] just couldn't resist. It was Mike's senior year in college, and the big football game was imminent. He was not a football player, but Mike wanted to do something unprecedented to help ensure victory. Although strictly prohibited, late one night Mike led a small group of fellow students through the off-limit tunnels beneath the college. They avoided detection and reached their goal: a small stairway that led to the roof of the student center.

Once on top of the building, they unfurled two large banners promoting school spirit and hung them over the edge so they would be clearly visible to all. As they put the banners in place, Mike could almost hear the admiring comments from his fellow students as they passed by. His accomplishment would be spoken of for years, even if no one ever knew for sure who was cool enough to pull it off.

---

1 Oswald Chambers, *My Utmost for His Highest*, October 17 (Grand Rapids, Michigan: Discovery House Publishers, 1992), 215.
2 Name and some details have been changed.

93

No doubt it would have been the great success he envisioned, except that in the darkness he failed to see the air ventilator shaft on the roof of the student center. Running at full speed, he fell into it and hit bottom approximately fifteen feet below.

When I first met Mike, he was a sorry sight standing there in my office with his broken arm in a sling and his broken jaw wired shut. My task was to defend Mike at the disciplinary board that was going to hear his case very soon. When I asked Mike what caused him to do something so stupid and put his entire future at risk, his confusion was clear. He said, "I just don't know why I did it…or what made me do it…I guess I just made a mistake."

The last thing Mike wanted that night on the roof was light; he was counting on the darkness of the night to hide him so he could avoid detection while on the rooftop. But that same darkness prevented him from seeing the airshaft. He had made a big mistake.

Keep Your Focus on the Future
Have you ever known someone who lives life looking in a rearview mirror, worrying about what was done wrong in the past? It is almost as if that person wears a ball and chain and can't break free. He can't move on and focus on the great things possible in the future because he is thinking about what he should have done better before.

In his letter to the Philippians, Paul cautions against making that mistake and encourages us to keep our minds on what lies ahead, on the potential of what is to come rather than worrying about what could have been better.

> …But one thing I do: Forgetting what is behind and straining toward what is ahead, I press on toward the goal to win the prize for which God has called me heavenward in Christ Jesus (Philippians 3:13–14 NIV).[3]

In verse 12 of the same chapter Paul says, "…I press on to take hold of that for which Christ Jesus took hold of me" (NIV).

---

3 Similarly, Isaiah 43:18 says, "Forget the former things; do not dwell on the past" (NIV).

When I was in the military, "press on" was a frequently used term meaning to keep moving forward and get through whatever was slowing you down. Someone might say, "Press on, Merrell," as a general encouragement. I started to use the term at home and with our friends, and it was great advice. If I hadn't learned to do this, my life could have become a tangle of guilt about yesterday with little focus on the future before me.

When I get discouraged, I usually discover that my failure to focus on the future is at the root of the problem. For example, as a parent it is easy for me to slip into the "if I had only done this better" way of thinking. At first I am thinking about one or two things I definitely messed up. But then I remember more and more of my mistakes, and if I'm not careful they become the only things I can recall, such as maybe I spoke too loudly to the kids in anger about unimportant things, like cleaning their room or hanging up their clothes.

Once I spent the weekend moving furniture and polishing the wood floors in our house. When I got home on Monday, I was shocked to see skid marks all across it. The kids had been playing a game and sliding across my newly waxed floor with their shoes on. I can't recall exactly what I said, but I do know that it was a mistake. My wife would probably call it yelling—and she would be right. At other times I didn't show consideration for my wife's input, so the kids saw us arguing instead of working together on a problem. And there were countless other mistakes I made.

As parents we make hundreds of decisions each year and are sure to get some of them wrong. What I have learned is that replaying prior decisions over in my mind and worrying about them does not change the outcome. If I am not careful, though, I'll begin to think about how much better it might have been if I had done things differently. I could worry myself into thinking I should not have been a parent at all!

Paul says it's too late to do anything about those prior mistakes now, and his counsel is to keep your focus on the future. If you ever catch yourself thinking, "If I had only done x instead of y," then you are forgetting Paul's instruction. God doesn't intend for you to live your life looking in the rearview mirror! Instead of thinking about the past, learn from your mistake and keep pressing on to find the wonderful things coming in the future. God is so great and what happens when you follow His Word is so perfect, you don't need to spend time looking over your shoulder. You'll be glad you kept your focus on the future.

Mistakes Happen
There will be times, though, when you realize that you have made a serious error that is continuing and you have to stop it. When that happens, you must repent and make a change. This is the teaching of Genesis 16:6–9 (NIV), when an angel found Hagar by a spring in the desert and asked where she was going. Hagar said, "I'm running away from my mistress Sarai." The angel told her, "Go back to your mistress and submit to her." Hagar was wrong to run away, so the angel told her to return home. One lesson being taught in this passage is, when you know you have done the wrong thing, admit it and correct it.

There is no way to anticipate everything that can go wrong in life, but there are at least three categories of serious patterns that should be avoided.

Mistake #1 – Repeating Sinful Patterns
You make a mistake when you repeat sinful behavior without realizing what you are doing. Those destructive patterns frequently originate within the family and are sometimes referred to as generational curses. For example, although I didn't realize it while I was growing up, a critical spirit set the pattern in our family. There were negative comments made when food wasn't quite salty enough or hot enough, or when the mowed grass looked nice but the trimming wasn't done perfectly. This habit had undoubtedly been passed on from one generation to the next, without anyone realizing the damage being inflicted. But in our family, nothing was ever quite good enough. Whether it was work, cooking, grades or friends, there seemed to be negative comments about everything.

After experiencing this negativity growing up, I realized later I was subconsciously doing the same thing to my own family.

Shortly after Cheri and I were married, we were serving pasta to some guests. Thinking the spaghetti was done, she poured out the boiling water and served it. It didn't take long to realize it was not done, which meant we had to wait until more water boiled so the next batch of pasta could be fully cooked. Acting on what I had seen growing up and not thinking about what I was saying, I began to make fun of her. I thought I was being funny, but our friends didn't think so and neither did Cheri! Over the following years this pattern continued and was being passed on to our kids. It is hard to believe how easy it is to do this. It was unknowingly done, and, if someone had asked, I would have denied doing anything wrong. But it was true; I had a critical spirit, and I was passing it on.

In the Sermon on the Mount, Jesus said,

> *Don't pick on people, jump on their failures, criticize their faults—unless, of course, you want the same treatment. That **critical spirit** has a way of boomeranging. It's easy to see a smudge on your neighbor's face and be oblivious to the ugly sneer on your own. Do you have the nerve to say, "Let me wash your face for you," when your own face is distorted by contempt? It's this whole traveling road-show mentality all over again, playing a holier-than-thou part instead of just living your part. Wipe that ugly sneer off your own face, and you might be fit to offer a washcloth to your neighbor* (Matthew 7:1–5 MSG, emphasis added).

In his translation of Matthew 7:1, J. B. Phillips puts it this way:

> *Don't criticise people, and you will not be criticised. For you will be judged by the way you criticise others, and the measure you give will be the measure you receive.*

It was while on the wilderness camping trip that I realized what I was doing. It happened after we had surrendered our watches (this was before cell phones) and were left alone in the woods to focus on Psalm 104 for an extended time. It was then I realized that my sin of criticism was being passed on through mindless repetition. And suddenly I knew I had to stop it! When I realized this, it was like a flash of lightning, and I was filled with sorrow for what I had been doing. I asked God to forgive me for the damage I had already inflicted on my wife and our kids, and when I got back home I asked the family for forgiveness.

I was confident I could break this generational curse, but when I began trying to change, I realized that it was very hard to kill the spirit of criticism. Notice I said "trying to change" because I found this to be a long-term process. Over time and with the help of my wife I have begun to put an end to this very damaging habit. Although from time to time I am still drawn back into making critical comments, most of the time I am able to resist the temptation to say negative things. I am not where I want to be, but I am improving by the grace of God.

Let me give another example. I worked with a man who was very articulate, and he used this skill to advance his career. On social occasions he would use his mastery of language to create and recite short rhyming verses, called limericks, which were frequently off-color. He did this for years, thinking it was innocent fun and unaware of the example he was setting. But as he got older, he realized the harm it was causing and decided to stop, cold turkey. He didn't want to be remembered as the "guy who told dirty jokes." It wasn't easy for him to make that change as he struggled to leave a positive, not a smutty, legacy. It is another example of how living an unexamined life can lead to mistakes and sin.

What does this mean for you? Think about your life critically, considering those things you could be repeating while unknowingly harming others. You may not mean to, but it has become a habit, and you could easily be inflicting pain on those you love most. How do you begin to set things right? As you become aware of a sinful pattern interfering with your life and relationships, you must do the hard work of recognizing and confessing your mistake and then making the necessary changes to set things right.

Mistake #2 – Violating God's Moral Laws

You have undoubtedly heard about the moral failures of high-pro-file preachers or people you thought were strong Christians. Those mistakes happen with some regularity. What can be done to rectify these and similar failures? Consider what you might do if you made a decision that violated God's moral laws. It could involve some aspect of your work, the amount of taxes you owe, your family or church life, or almost anything else. It is not hard to become a slave to sin, but it goes without saying that you should never willingly step into sin. What should you do if you make a mistake leading to sinful behavior? To clarify this, let me give you an example.

While I was in law school, I enjoyed courses in constitution-al law. In addition to the required course, I took two additional courses: criminal constitutional law and freedom of speech. I was captivated by the United States Supreme Court reinterpreting the law in certain areas and by the opinions of its most liberal jus-tices. During this time, the court watched movies to determine if they were pornographic or not. If the film was pornographic, then it was not protected by the first amendment and its exhibi-tion could be halted and its creators prosecuted. Because I had gone to the Air Force Academy, I was committed to work for the Air Force, but otherwise I would likely have taken a job with a group seeking to liberalize such expression. Of course, I will never be sure, but I could have been enticed into legal work pro-moting the pornographic industry. I am eternally thankful I did not have that temptation, but if I had become involved, it would have been in violation of God's moral law.

Sin usually starts small and grows over time, and it can become a permanent part of your life. If your choices have led you into a situation in which you are violating God's moral law, you must immediately make a change, ask for forgiveness and begin to live your life as God directs. As Oswald Chambers said, "Every once in a while our Lord gives us a glimpse of what we would be like if it were not for Him. This is a confirmation of what he said—'Without me you can do nothing.'"[4] (See John 15:5.)

---

4 Oswald Chambers, My Utmost for His Highest, December 23 (Grand Rapids, Michigan: Discovery House Publishers, 1992), 266.

Mistake #3 – Fearing Change
It may be difficult to determine if a change would improve some aspect of your life. Would things be better if you made a change? Many people are afraid to even consider the possibility because they believe that what they have, no matter how bad, is probably better than what they might end up with after making a change. How many times have people failed to move from a good situation to a great one because of the possibility of failure?[5] But if all things work together for good, why should you be afraid of making a change if you believe it would be beneficial? If you are stuck in a job or a place or a situation that leaves you feeling hopeless or alone, why not take steps to consider a change?

In First Corinthians 7:21 Paul says, "Were you a slave when you were called? Don't let it trouble you—although if you can gain your freedom, do so" (NIV). This means you are free to change your vocation.[6] Here is the key: be content with your life, but if you can improve your situation, then you are free to do it. If you have a sense of overall contentment about where you are living and what you are doing, just continue doing it. But if you feel that you are in the wrong job and it could be time to make a change, why not consider it?

You might wonder whether there is something bigger in your future, and you would like to find out what it could be. First evaluate whether your current responsibilities allow you to make a change without disrupting things at work, unnecessarily uprooting your family or similar concerns. Then allow things to develop as you seek alternative work, most likely in your community. If you have a strong desire to make a more dramatic change, such as moving to a new town or returning to school, then you could look into those possibilities as well. You can serve the Lord and trust that things will work out for good as you make changes.

---

5 Jim Collins, *Good to Great: Why Some Companies Make the Leap and Others Don't* (New York, New York: Harper Collins Publishers, 2001).

6 For a much fuller discussion of this topic, see Friesen, *Decision Making*, 199 and 345 ("If it does not otherwise violate the moral law of God, the opportunity for vocational change or advancement may be taken").

Personal Experience (Part 4)

Having made many moves and other changes throughout my life, I have found it liberating to consider change and not be limited by the thought that I might somehow fail or upset God's will for me. Following my graduation from Moody's Biblical Studies masters' program, we were living and working in Virginia. My wife, as always, quickly found a job with the public schools and I was working as an assistant superintendent at a large Christian school. When I took the job, I was pretty sure I would enjoy it because both of our families were involved with education (we had one high school principal, two teachers, a school secretary and a speech therapist). There was just one problem: I did not like it at all. In fact, the longer I was there, the more I realized that I was not cut out for the job. It seemed to me there were too many long meetings, and each meeting was a rehash of what had been discussed the week before. Worst of all, it took a very long time to reach and implement a decision. I was so frustrated that I put this Bible verse up in large letters on my office bulletin board:

...Monthly conferences, weekly Sabbaths, special meetings—meetings, meetings, meetings—I can't stand one more! Meetings for this, meetings for that. I hate them! You've worn me out! (Isaiah 1:13–14 MSG)

People chuckled when they saw it, but after I had worked there for about one year it finally hit me that I had made a mistake. Despite it being a good job at an excellent school, I knew that I needed to make a change. At one of our frequent staff meetings among the superintendent and his assistants, I surprised myself by saying I would be leaving the school at the end of the semester. They asked me what I would be doing, and I said, "I will continue to serve the Lord." But I had no idea what would be next.

I then found positions with two large ministries located in Colorado Springs, both of which my wife and I loved. Since Cheri was born in nearby Denver and her family lived there, I was hoping she might be willing to leave her very good position in

Virginia to go back home. I was looking for a position that would allow me to get back to what I was good at: the law.

One of the ministries was seeking someone with legal experience to work on international intellectual property matters. I knew very little about that kind of legal work but applied anyway. The position was in the legal department, and it was first advertised the day I saw it. I don't know how many others applied, but after a lengthy application process I was offered the job. My wife was more than happy to head back home, and so we moved to Colorado.

What about not looking back? I had not been satisfied with my job in education and felt that I needed a change. I was not looking for a special sign from God, or a hidden message in Scripture, or the opinion of my friends. I took the new job, but as I started work it quickly became apparent how much I had to learn. Shortly after I started, one of my co-workers asked, "Why did we hire someone who knows so little about what we do?" Embarrassed by such a good question and not having an answer, I began a diligent study of intellectual property law. It was a steep learning curve, but I improved, worked hard and developed great relationships with the international department employees. I even received occasional thank-you notes for my work—something quite rare for an attorney!

I had some ideas about changes to improve the department's overall efficiency and made some suggestions, but I was told that I should keep my focus on the work I had been hired to do. I accepted my limited role, taking comfort from the Scripture's story of Korah, a Levite who rebelled against Moses while seeking a greater role for himself. Moses said to him,

> Isn't it enough for you that the God of Israel has separated you from the rest of the Israelite community and brought you near himself to do the work at the LORD's tabernacle and to stand before the community and minister to them? He has brought you and all your fellow Levites near himself, but now you are trying to get the priesthood too (Numbers 16:9–10 NIV).

I always started work early, well before the official workday began. After I had been working for about six months, I was at my desk early one morning when my office phone rang. It was the supervisor of my immediate boss, a man I had met only once when I started work. He asked me to come to his office, and after some small talk he surprised me by asking if I would like to become the leader of the legal department. I told him I would be honored to take the assignment, but I felt overwhelmed by this sudden and unexpected request. I was also concerned about how the other employees in the department would react. Some of them had been there for years and knew a lot more about intellectual property than I ever would. Thankfully, however, the change went well, and we all continued to work together.

For the next five years I served the ministry during a turbulent time that included the departure of the ministry's founder. It wasn't always pleasant, but I knew that I was in the right place at the right time. The circumstances had been intimidating, and with the change I felt like I was stepping off a cliff with nothing below to stop my fall. But I put my faith in the Lord and took a step into the unknown future. Whenever I have done that, it has become easier to do it the next time.

Of course, there have been mistakes I have made about job changes. At one time when I was between jobs, I convinced myself that I had a future as a photographer. I always liked taking photos and had a nice camera, and there was a coffee shop not far from where we lived that let patrons sell their photographs. I had some of my favorite photos framed and added them to the collection there, expecting to get a call from someone (with good taste) who wanted to buy one. I priced them at rock-bottom prices and waited for a call. Finally, after two months had passed without any interest, I concluded that photography was not the career for me.

You don't have to be tied down or wait for a secret signal from God that the time is right for a change. You can do it now while continuing to count on the Lord to bring good out of it. In short, you can experience God's will by living your life freely as you work to bring glory to His name, so long as you are within His moral law. And you can enjoy His marvelous promise of an open and spacious life.

Heavenly Father,

We praise You today as the God of second chances who knows us intimately. You know when we are on a path leading us off track. When that happens, we ask that You to make it clear to us and give us the wisdom and grace to respond in a way that pleases You. Allow us to repent and move into the free and spacious life You promise, fueled with endless energy and boundless strength to do Your will.

We ask this in the precious name of Jesus, amen.

Chapter Ten

GO WHERE YOU NEVER DREAMED

They [the righteous] *will bear fruit even when old and gray; they will remain lush and fresh in order to proclaim: "The* LORD *is righteous. He's my rock...."*
—Psalm 92:14–15 (CEB)

One summer while on vacation at the beach, we noticed that a large crowd had gathered near the ocean. It was just after sunset on a warm August evening, and our family went down to investigate the commotion. About a hundred little sea turtles, each of them only a little larger than a silver dollar, had just hatched and were burrowing out of their nest at the edge of the sand dunes, about fifteen yards from the ocean. Blind at birth, they can sense only brightness, and so they instinctively follow the light reflecting off the sea that leads them into the water.

But due to the competing glimmer of lights on the shore and the brightness of the nearby city, many of the hatchlings seemed to be confused. Instead of heading toward the ocean, they were crawling onto the sand dunes where they would face certain death in the heat and sun the next morning. The glow of the light on the ocean simply was not as bright as the artificial light that was leading them in the wrong direction.

At the suggestion of a local resident who had seen this happen before, we all ran back to our beach houses, grabbed flashlights and returned.[1] Dozens of us stood ankle deep in the surf and focused our flashlight beams on the little turtles. What happened next was truly amazing!

One by one they turned, drawn by the bright light we shined on them, from the dryness of the sand and toward the life-giving ocean. Not all of them turned, but most did. We then watched them stumble clumsily across the sand until they reached the water, where they were transformed from unstable land mammals into strong swimmers as they reached the habitat they were designed for. We helped lead them from confusion to life that is rich and full.

The recurring message throughout this book is that as you delight in the Lord and act on the new desires God implants in you, all things in your life will work together for good as you are conformed to the image of Christ. The way this happens is usually a surprise. It is a wonderful gift from a good God, and it is better, bigger and bolder than you imagined. You will find that your best years are ahead of you, and things will culminate in joy as your abilities are fully used in ways you never dreamed. Instead of being led toward a false light, you will find yourself in the wonderful waters of God's love.

Think about the story of Moses.[2] When he was a boy, he was raised in the palace of Pharaoh, but he was forced to flee to Midian as a young man. For the next forty years he tended sheep, but then, when he least expected it, God told Moses that he would be the one who would lead Israel out of Egypt and into the promised land. Moses was surprised by this, and at the age of eighty was reluctant to serve. Finally he obeyed God, and for the next forty years led the Israelites through the wilderness. This is a wonderful example of how God will use skills and abilities developed over the years to repurpose the life of someone willing to serve Him.[3]

---

1 This event happened years ago, long before the rules about how best to deal with hatchlings were adopted.

2 See Exodus chapter 2 and Acts 7:30 (NIV).

3 Second Chronicles 16:9a says, "For the eyes of the Lord range throughout the earth to strengthen those whose hearts are fully committed to him" (NIV).

Personal Experience (Part 5)
Becoming a Professor

Up to 2010 my life had been somewhat predictable. I practiced law for thirty years, attended Moody, and became the head of the legal department for a Christian ministry. Things were going well and I was satisfied, but what happened next could not have been foreseen. It was far outside of my expectations. God was working all things for good, but I had no idea what was about to happen.

After five years with the Christian ministry in Colorado, I knew that my service was complete and it was time to leave. I was confident that I would find another position and had no intention of retiring. For many years Cheri and I had dreamed of living at the beach, and we moved to South Carolina. Cheri quickly found a job in the public schools of Myrtle Beach, and I was still looking for one. We lived near Litchfield Beach in Pawleys Island, which is beautiful—it is on the Atlantic Ocean sixty miles north of Charleston, South Carolina, and twenty-five miles south of Myrtle Beach—a wonderful place to live.

The beach is serene for nine months out of the year and packed with beach lovers the other three months. We enjoyed both seasons. There was a community feeling among the permanent residents, and we found a great church. I also operated a nonprofit that offered Christian-based mediation services. Over the years, however, that business had only three clients, and all three ultimately decided not to mediate their dispute. My efforts as an entrepreneur were a complete failure! I also applied for a position as general counsel at a very large, well-known Christian ministry. I thought that with my experience working for the ministry in Colorado Springs, I should have a good chance of getting the job. It was a highly sought-after position, however, and there were several other attorneys who also applied. To make a long story short, I did not get the job. I was frustrated and couldn't think of any alternatives for my next job.

An attorney representing nonprofits nationwide knew about my situation and sent me the names of Christian companies looking for an additional attorney. I applied with a few of them but received rejections from all of them. I remember one that was particularly painful. I would have been the fifth lawyer in a five-person department, and when I spoke to the lawyer in charge, he was very encouraging. I submitted my application and then I waited…and waited…but I never heard anything from that ministry at all! I didn't even get a rejection—just silence. At sixty-five I thought maybe I was too old, but I couldn't really believe that since my granddad had worked until he was eighty-five. I was in good health and felt younger than my real age.[4] My new company had failed, I couldn't land a job, and I began to wonder if things were not going to work out. My wife and I had left our secure jobs in Colorado to go to a place we had never lived before and where we didn't know anyone. What I thought would be my next career had not materialized. I started to think, "What could I have done differently?" My plans for what might happen next had failed, and I worried that there might not be anything else for me.

It was at this point that I realized instead of looking to see what lay ahead, I had begun to think about what I could have done differently. I knew using the words, "could have done" meant that I was on the wrong track, but I didn't know what else to do. I am sorry to say I found myself looking back, while the path forward was going to involve something new and different.

At Pawleys Island one of our neighbors was a Christian couple who had two children. As we got to know them, we found out that the woman, who I'll call Jill, was an adjunct professor at the local, secular community college where she taught classes in comparative world religions. Jill told me that she was going to leave her position that summer to become a public school teacher. Her position at the college would soon be open, and she encouraged me to apply for her job. I submitted an application and was asked to come in for an interview with the department head, which lasted about ten minutes.

When the interview was over, the department head told me that I had the job and would start in the fall semester. I was amazed and silently wondered, "What just happened?" Suddenly my life was turned upside down and headed in a totally unexpected

---

4 Michael F. Roizen, *Real Age: Are You As Young As You Can Be?* (New York: Cliff Street Books, an imprint of Harper-Collins Publishers, 1999).

direction. The new job would allow me to influence hundreds of college students at a critical time in their lives. I had never thought about the possibility of becoming a professor, but suddenly I had the opportunity to step into that role. I got busy preparing for class with outlines, notes and tests. Sometimes my preparation was only a couple of lessons ahead of what we were studying.

The question I had to resolve was how to teach my classes. In world religions at the college level, students are frequently encouraged to question religion and God. Some professors emphasize what is happening on the world stage to explain that religion is a man-made response to outside events. Others love Eastern religions, like Buddhism, and teach primarily about those ideas. Others downplay Christianity, teaching that all religions worship the same spirit and result in the same thing at the end of life. I found out that many students avoided taking a religion course because they were afraid the professor would make fun of their beliefs.

I wondered whether I could teach the course in a way that advanced Christianity, and as I worked on my presentations, I became convinced that this would not be difficult to do. I decided to focus on what each major religion believed without mentioning my Christian beliefs. When the beliefs of other religions are placed side by side with Christianity, it becomes obvious it is true and the others false.

For example, I think that Hinduism is one of the most depressing religions imaginable. It has thousands of gods, ceremonies with no meaning, a text with no known authors, and demeaning beliefs about the caste system. It also promotes the concept of reincarnation, but not the idealized fantasy Westerners usually hold. People here want to believe that in a prior life they were Joan of Arc, Teddy Roosevelt or someone equally well known. To the contrary, Hindus view reincarnation negatively, believing that they have already lived hundreds or thousands of lives with endless cycles of death and rebirth. They just want the cycle to stop as they finally reach the end of their suffering, which they call nirvana. In nirvana their lives are blown out like a candle and their suffering finally ends.

If I presented the beliefs of each religion side by side, then most students would inevitably conclude that Christianity was true. It stands out among the world's religions and doesn't need a defense in an academic setting. My biggest difficulty was that a number of students were secularists who did not believe in any higher being. That group was troubling because many didn't care about anything except having a good time, and as a result they didn't take the class seriously. With that exception, however, my approach was successful, and I was very happy with my decision.

Not once had I ever thought about becoming a college professor, but God provided the opportunity for me to teach about a hundred students each semester. It was a job I did not expect and it came about in an unusual way. It was not the result of a clever plan on my part; I got the job because God was working everything in my life for good. I realized that I had become qualified as a college professor through my three years as a member of the faculty at the Air Force Academy early in my career, then by working at the school in Virginia, and finally by getting a master's degree at Moody. Those events were separated by more than twenty-five years! There is beauty and wonder at seeing how God brought those experiences together and provided the opportunity for me to use them to His glory. Who knows how I might have influenced my students or what the impact of my teaching might be? I am waiting with anticipation to find the answer to that question in heaven.

God is all-powerful, and you should trust Him to work your diverse interests and experiences into His plans. Those plans will be for your good, and they will become part of God's much bigger plan to advance His kingdom here on earth. It will not be what you expect and may be a complete surprise using gifts and abilities you did not realize you had. You will see that God is using your life to bless others, and things will fall into place in miraculous ways as you use your desires to bring glory to His name.

Personal Experience (Part 6)
Becoming an Author
We have all been forced to stay at home and in masks for almost three years as a result of the Covid pandemic. It has not been

enjoyable, and it has lasted a lot longer than expected. It was difficult to visit our families, and even now there is no assurance that something is not coming next.

Finding a silver lining in that event is not easy, but the pandemic has forced us to find other interests and ways of doing things. For example, some people have reached the conclusion that they can work more efficiently from home, which has transformed workplaces. Others have become less sociable in person, but they have developed a robust online presence. It has given me time to write this book. I thought about writing some time ago, but I concluded that there are too many books available already. So why would I write, especially a book on a difficult, non-fiction, Christian topic? I am unknown and too inexperienced to start a writing career.

The concept for writing this book began when we were visiting my hometown of Charleston, West Virginia. I talked with a friend during the pandemic who suggested I should write a book about my experiences. She said since I had held so many jobs, had lived many places, and had an unusual perspective on God's will, that I should share my story. Initially I didn't give it much thought, but then I began to wonder, "What if this might become a new part of my story? What if, while we are locked up waiting for a solution to the pandemic, this could be a way for God to be glorified through me?" Of course, at the same time I also heard another voice asking, "What if you can't get it published? What if you can't write anything relevant to others?" To be honest, I wasn't sure what I should do. I talked with Cheri and some friends about it. I prayed about it. I finally decided to go ahead and write the book. Notice I didn't say I "would try" to do it. That thought plants seed of doubt and is like saying "I'm not sure, but I will start and just see how it goes." If you do that, you will never actually write a book, which takes time, determination and commitment. I like what Yoda said: "Try not. Do or do not. There is no try."[5]

To get started, I looked back through various papers and notes I kept, and I realized that I had been studying and teaching about

---

5 Yoda to Luke Skywalker, *Star Wars Episode V: The Empire Strikes Back*, film, directed by Irvin Kershner, 1980.

God's will for years, ever since my wife and I taught our daughter's eighth grade Sunday school class years ago. I still have the page we distributed, entitled "Finding God's Plan for Your Life." I have read many books on the topic and taught a seminar at the Christian school in Virginia. Some of the most useful information came from the list I kept of significant events in my life, which I called "Seeing God's Hand of Blessing on My Life." As I looked back over what happened, it was apparent that God had miraculously brought all things together for good throughout my life.

I became convinced that I should write this book and simply trust that everything else about getting it published, distributed and accepted by readers would take care of itself. Writing it has been much more time-consuming and difficult than I expected. I encountered questions such as these: How long should it be? What style should I use in writing it? Would anyone help me as I began to write, edit and get it ready for publication?[6] How should I organize it? How could I find the answers to those questions? Does the story make sense?

There is a lot in this book about my life because I believe that I had these various experiences in order to enable me to write it. Some may think there is too much about me in this book, but my story is really about God—about delighting in Him and growing in Him—and of seeing throughout all the experiences of life He has been with me. Through the good times and the bad, the bright days and the cloudy days, through good health and illness—in short, through all the experiences of life, God has been there. God has worked all things in my life for good by conforming me more into the image of Christ. And the beauty of all of this is, He will do it for you, too! He is waiting, willing and able to do the same thing for anyone who seeks it. And as you go through life, you can look back and see God's mercy and grace are "new every morning" (Lamentations 3:23 NIV).

Cheri and I saw our lives change once we gave up being "minor league" Christians and became increasingly dedicated to serving God. We saw what happened after we turned up the volume of

6 A special thank you is in order to Chris Fabry and Keith Carroll, who have helped me with this book in so many ways.

our Christian homing beacon so we could again clearly hear God. When we joined a church that preached the gospel and all that Jesus has done, we grew. As we read the Bible each day, we grew. When I attended Promise Keepers events, my faith exploded, leading us to eventually sell our home of fourteen years and move to Chicago to attend Moody Theological Seminary. We saw how the time working as an assistant superintendent at the school in Virginia compelled me to look for another job, only to find it on the same day it was first advertised. That resulted in me becoming the director of the legal department at a large Christian ministry. We also found real blessing in being near Cheri's parents while living in Colorado. It was during this time that the new ministry of Possibilities Africa started and began to grow slowly, with people from all over the world playing a part in its growth. Then when we got to South Carolina, I became a religion professor teaching hundreds of college students. And now this book has been the latest surprise for me.

I wrote this book to share these stories with you in the hope that they would:

- provide a different and more effective way for you to experience the will of God in your life;
- inspire and motivate you to believe that you can live a free and open life as God promises;
- help you find fulfillment and meaning as you live your life with purpose and without fear that you might miss God's will;
- allow you to see you are living in God's will right now—the life right in front of you—and
- help you realize that you don't have to be a scholar or a professional to make this happen. It can happen now.

First I was an Air Force lawyer, next a lawyer in private practice, then a lawyer working for a Christian ministry, a professor, and most recently an author. Who could have foreseen it? How could it all have happened? Yet, it did. These opportunities have come together in my life and are wonderful blessings. But of course, God is really the star of my story because the miraculous path I followed is the result of something much bigger than I am. As I trusted God and delighted myself in Him, He gave me the desires of my heart and wove them into a story beyond belief. He did it for me as I trusted Him each step of the way.

What about you? For years the Army had a slogan saying, "Be all you can be," which seems like good advice. But there is so much more that God can do in and through your life. After all, it is not about you, but God. There are opportunities waiting that you can experience once you realize your freedom in Christ. You embrace God's desires, and then, as you implement them, you can watch God work to expand your horizons beyond anything you thought possible. What can you be? What can you do? How can you use it all to glorify God, being open to the opportunities He provides?

Don't wait for a special sign to begin; start now to serve Him and continue throughout your life. You'll be glad you did.

Heavenly Father,

Thank You for surprises in our lives and for giving us new opportunities to serve You. Only You can take what seems to be a dead end and miraculously change it into a wonderful new opportunity to serve You. We praise You for trusting us to grow in ways we never considered and to accomplish the tasks set before us. We pray that You will allow us to influence others in ways that bring glory to Your name, so that at the end of our lives we can look back and see how each step has led to the next in a beautiful tapestry woven by Your gracious hand.

In the name of Jesus, amen.

Chapter Eleven

HOW TO SEE WHAT GOD HAS DONE

Let this be written down for the next generation so that people not yet created will praise the LORD.
                    —Psalm 102:18 (CEB)

We know that God is constantly working in our lives, but some people miss that fact simply because they haven't thought about a way to track the miraculous events that happen years apart. How can you be sure to realize what God has been doing throughout your life?

Begin by thinking about trying to solve a mystery and ask, "What would Sherlock Holmes do?" You know those famous detective stories. He always does the same things. First he stays alert, watching the suspects and noticing clues. Next he reviews his notes about what he has found, and finally he makes deductions that solve the case. In a similar way, you can see God working by following that approach. It won't take a lot of time, but is essential in order to grasp the full picture of what God has done. Let's look at what you need to do, when you should get started, and what the end result will look like.

Keep a List

To see how God has been working in your life, start by making a list of what has happened to you that seems significant in some way. This sounds simple, so simple perhaps you might be inclined to skip it and just try to recall the information later, but that won't work. Instead, think back and recall those events that easily come to mind. What kind of family and childhood did you have? Where did you live? Were your relatives nearby? Did you like school, what clubs were you in, or what was your favorite subject? Then move on to your teen years, college life and so on.

As you do this, some events will strike you as significant, and when that happens, write them down. Wait a few days, then go back through your list, adding things that you overlooked. Also include events that seem to be insignificant but are repeated or have an impact on later events. Feel free to revise your list as you recall additional items. Continue to record events as they happen over the years, always looking for patterns. Write them down in the order they happened, and as you do you will most likely recall other significant or seemingly unusual events in your life. The idea is to include as many of these events as possible.

When to Get Started

The earlier you start keeping track, the easier it will be, but you can begin at any age. The primary reason for starting young is because the big picture of what God is doing becomes clearer as you age. Try not to overlook an important piece of information that could be forgotten, since if it is recorded it might clarify what happens later. If you do this, you will begin to see how seemingly unrelated events fit together.

You should make regular entries and keep them up to date. Your list doesn't need to be complicated; the point is to write things down in the order they happen. If you have only a vague memory of an important event, a relative might be able to assist you with getting the facts straight.

As you do this, encourage your immediate family to do the same. They may be reluctant to get started, but when they see what the list provides, it will be easier to get them on board. Help your children beginning around age ten or twelve years old. If you convince them to get started while young, they will thank you later. Every six months or so, talk with your kids and family about what you have seen God doing in their lives. Help them start a basic list they can add to as the years pass. Keep it simple and enjoyable and show them the list you have been keeping.

What It Could Look Like

I have included a portion of the list I have kept over the years to give you an idea of what your list might look like.

Seeing God's Hand of Blessing on My Life

- Grew up in a Christian home with Dad who was a principal and Mom who stayed at home with my sisters and me.
- Admitted to the USAF Academy / despite having to take the glucose tolerance test twice and having no team sport experience / not getting into the AF masters' program due to airsickness and instead going to law school.
- Meeting and marrying Cheri / her roommate was dating my roommate / growing with her in our commitment to the Lord over the years / her amazing way of getting a new job with the schools in every place we lived, and always smiling.
- Going to law school at Vanderbilt / getting a scholarship to attend / gaining confidence.
- Having first job in the AF JAG corps / teaching law at AFA.
- Leaving the Air Force JAG corps and getting a job at a law firm in West Virginia / finding a Christian counselor who helped me believe I could make a change.
- Deciding to leave the law firm and move to Birmingham, Alabama, with a Fortune 500 company.
- Returning from Alabama to West Virginia to take general counsel job at the bank for fourteen years while kids were in school / joining the reserves and eventually retiring from the AF / getting promoted to Lt. Colonel despite lack of professional military education.

- Having and raising the kids / becoming involved with Promise Keepers and more involved with church / determining to quit being critical of others / hearing about Promise Keepers and through it transforming my life.
- Hearing through a conference about tithing, leading to a change in our giving.
- Cheri's surgery and depression followed by joy as she volunteered at the hospital to help others / rather than being bitter she used the experience for good, as a benefit to others.
- Wanting to do whatever it took to dedicate the second half of my life to serving God / going to Moody Bible Institute and getting a masters' degree / going to work at a Christian school in Virginia.
- Meeting Martin Simiyu on first mission trip in 2002 and helping start the ministry of Possibilities Africa / seeing the amazing combination of people who made it successful over the years.
- Getting a job at a ministry in Colorado and working during a time of change of outside general counsel and retirement of founder / being selected to lead the legal department after six months.
- Seeing our daughter decide to go to Africa for six months as a Christian volunteer to help kids, which led to Cheri being willing to go to Africa with me to visit Possibilities Africa.
- Moving to Pawleys Island, South Carolina / not getting the job as general counsel with another ministry / no mediation business / getting hired as a professor of religion at a local secular college / teaching at AFA played a key role in my getting this position.
- Moving to Charlotte, North Carolina, and then to Hackettstown, New Jersey, both moves to accompany daughter to her new jobs / while in Charlotte volunteered at the hospital after hip surgery based on Cheri's experience volunteering years before in West Virginia.

- Not being able to do anything during Covid, deciding to write a book about God's will.
- Illnesses: torn meniscus (which led to six weeks on crutches) 2010 / Guillain-Barré Syndrome 2010 / hip replacement 2017 / hernia repair 2019 / detached retina 2023 / all making me more caring and understanding of the needs of others and ultimately reflecting the image of Christ more fully.

Notice this is primarily a list of the things that have happened in my life, but it also includes a few statements reflecting how God used these events. Begin to think over these things in your life, looking for what God has done and how all of it has been working for good. I have been keeping this list for years and have added things that happened early in my life when what happened later showed their significance. You might think that you could just remember what happened, but for maximum effectiveness these events should be written down as they happen. Otherwise, you will likely forget or overlook some things or fail to see how they fit together.

For example, I initially forgot to include my promotion in the Air Force, which allowed me to continue in service until I reached retirement age. That came about in part because of an acquaintance I had made years before. If I hadn't known that officer, who later served as the head of my promotion board, I would have most likely been discharged before reaching twenty years of service, which is required for retirement pay. So I added that to my list and saw how it fit; its impact was immense. As a result of the retirement pay, I am able to serve God more fully now.

Later look for patterns in how the events listed worked together. Don't worry about whether you get things right; just try out various thoughts to see what develops. This might be the best aspect of getting older. You know the saying, "We're not getting older; we're getting better." When you are young and looking ahead, you might not be able to see how things fit together. But as years pass and you look back over your life, you can see more clearly and give thanks for what God has done. God provides increased perspective with age so you can see how He has worked things out in ways you could never have expected. Ask yourself, "How else could these apparent coincidences be understood? How else could they have happened?"

Let me give you another example of how apparently unrelated events happening years apart reveal a God who is orchestrating all things for good. While we lived in Pawleys Island, my parents lived not far away in Charleston, West Virginia. When they reached their eighties, their health began to deteriorate. My sister, who was living in the same town, handled most of their needs and took responsibility for being their primary caregiver. Still, I wanted to be there as often as possible and was able to make numerous trips to visit during their last years.

At times Dad recognized me and at other times he didn't, which was very difficult to deal with. Mom was coherent up to the end, which was a real blessing. At eighty-five years old, they died a few months apart. It was painful but a relief at the same time. Knowing that each of them had a strong Christian faith made their deaths more of a celebration than a time of sadness. As I later looked back at this experience, however, I could see how God was working:

- We were in Pawleys Island when my parents' health began to fail and they eventually died. I cannot imagine how much more difficult it would have been if we had been living over 1,300 miles away in Colorado. I could not have managed to visit them nearly as often as I did while living in nearby South Carolina.
- During these times of difficulty, I learned to be more patient, to have more empathy for those in need, and to honor my parents.

You, too, will see how God has brought people and events into your life that have been a blessing. You will become aware of things you have been able to do for the Lord. They don't have to be big or holy or significant events; instead, they could be routine and ordinary. But as you look back, you will begin to see how God has used them in a powerful way.

This will give you confidence when you feel like you are stepping off a cliff into the next phase of life. You won't be burdened by that fear, but instead you will know the wonderful freedom God provides while working all things together for good. With that assurance, you don't have to worry about each step you take. Instead, you freely move on to the next step, confident in what God has done in the past and knowing He will do it again. Always remember, as you take a step, you see the next.

Consider a Chart
I also suggest that you keep track of other items by using a chart. It should have the date and a very abbreviated listing of the things happening that year. In this chart you would add things like significant birthdays, purchases of houses, trips, changes at work, major illnesses, etc. Keeping a chart will make it easier to see events that don't seem significant at the time, but when seen in the bigger pattern, could be important. It might look something like this:

Big Chart – Travel and Moves

1972 (AFA) Nashville Married Cheri	1973	1974 (dog)	1975 (25 y.o.) (Vandy) Move to Rantoul, IL	1976
1977 (son born)	1978 Colorado Springs #1 home	1979	1980 (daughter born)	1981 (left AF) (J&K) Chas. WV, #2 home
1982	1983	1984	1985 (new company) Birmingham #3 home	1986 (bank) Charleston, WV #4 home
1987	1988	1989 (dog died)	1990	1991 (new dog)
1992 (20th Anniversary)	1993	1994	1995	1996
1997 Attend Promise Keepers conf.	1998 Spain w/ Armando	1999 Mcls 50th at Greenbrier hotel	2000 (50 y.o.) Left bank employment	2001 Moody GS Chicago

Look back at these lists from time to time to recall what happened and see the patterns that emerge. You may see "small" things that happened years before now becoming important pieces of a bigger picture. You may see how things that seemed insignificant, when considered in light of something happening later, were a part of what God brought together into a bigger picture. Trust the Lord when things take time and don't seem to be working out; you have to rest in Him and His timing, for He will work all things together for good.

When you get started in life, you probably have a plan in mind. But as life happens, you may end up living somewhere or doing something completely different than you imagined. If you had been told about it earlier you might have said, "That will never happen."

In my life, I would never have thought I could end up as a college professor of comparative world religions. But then in thinking back, I saw how God had worked the circumstances in my life in a miraculous way. All of those things happened so I could step in and teach hundreds of students about God, students who might otherwise have been taught by a secular atheist. How could this have happened unless God had been working all things for good? How else could I have been given the opportunity to be a blessing to so many? What a God we serve.

Faith Statement

Another way to begin to understand how God has been working in your life is to write a personal faith statement declaring what you believe and why. I have printed mine here as an example of what a faith statement might look like and to help get you started. Yours could be longer or shorter with more or less detail, but it should explain your faith journey and the impact it has had on your life. Your faith statement will be useful as an evangelism tool, as a reminder of what God has done in your life, or as an encouragement for future generations.

While at the Air Force Academy, I learned that to keep a plane flying on course, its radar must be set on the homing signal at its destination. *As long as that signal is followed, you cannot get lost, regardless of bad weather or other distractions. That has been true in my life as well.*

Although Cheri and I were experiencing worldly success, my legal job was demanding and life was becoming more complex. I was raised in a Christian home and had accepted Christ as my personal Savior, but I began to think of faith as just religion. We were slowly becoming conformed to the image of the world. I never turned off my "Christian homing signal," but there was increasing interference on my personal radar. As I strayed off course, peace seemed elusive and friendships shallow. I was becoming consumed by the demands of work, which left little time for the really important things in life. In short, things looked good from the outside, but inside my life was out of balance.

Then our teenage son and I attended an outdoor Christian wilderness camp, and as a result of that trip I heard about a new ministry called Promise Keepers. Along with 70,000 other men, I attended one of their first conferences and realized how far I had drifted off course. My Christian homing signal was re-calibrated, and I became involved in Bible study, prayer and small group accountability.

I felt like a man coming out of the desert, and I understood what Jesus meant when He said, "Whoever drinks the water I give them will never thirst" (John 4:14 NIV). My wife and I began to tune out the distractions of the world, and the results were amazing. As we trusted God with our finances, careers, children and future, things really began to change—all for the better and beyond what we could have imagined just a few years before.

My personal relationship with Jesus Christ provides me with a sense of wholeness that can't be found anywhere else. It gives me a desire to grow in the image of Christ and has miraculously freed me from my dependence upon status and security, instead providing the time and circumstances for full-time service.

My prayer is that you, too, will see the power and peace that can only come from faith in Christ and trust God as you seek significance through Him. God will provide the true desires of your heart and the motivation to share the joy only He can provide. God opened my heart in a wonderful way to feel compassion for others, and I am excited about what God will do through me in the future.

Practical Exercise

To assist you in tracing God's miracles, you might want to try a time line. Following is an abbreviated time line for a hypothetical man named Fred. Fred is young and has been writing down the things that have happened in his life. See if you can put the apparently random events into an order that shows how God is working all things in Fred's life for his good.

2006 – Graduated from high school / Loved studying Spanish / Admitted to the following colleges—Penn State, Denver University, Centenary University, Northampton Community College / Ambition to become a lawyer

2007 – Attended Northampton Community College to save money / Faith is growing / Ambition is changing—maybe become a preacher? / Dating a couple of girls

2010 – Finished community college and went to seminary / Finished undergraduate degree in biblical studies / Getting married to Kimberly next year

2015 – Finished graduate school with a degree in ministry / 1st child, Donnie, born / Has been contacted by a church in Puerto Rico to become its pastor

2019 – Moved to Honduras / In charge of a mission there

As you trace the significant events in Fred's life, you will come to appreciate that they were orchestrated by God into the patterns you see. For example, in the list you can see how Fred's interest in Spanish was used by God later in his life as he began serving in Spanish-speaking nations. My suggestion is that you start a list today and watch what God is doing in your life.

Heavenly Father,

We acknowledge that we are made in Your image and thank You for giving us dominion over all the earth. Today we especially thank You for the gift of our logical minds that allow us to sense eternity and our future. We also thank You for our intelligence and ask that You allow us to use our minds as we gain insight into the unique story of our lives. Let us track the patterns that emerge and see the bits and pieces, many of which may seem insignificant, as they come together in our lives and into the story that You are working out for our good. We thank You for giving each of us insight into how You are working the details of our lives into beautiful portraits of Your love. Let us live our lives in such a way that we bring glory and honor to Your name.

We pray in the precious name of Your Son, Jesus, amen.

Chapter Twelve

MORE QUESTIONS (PART 2)

Their teaching only causes useless guessing games instead of faithfulness to God's way of doing things.[1]
—1 Timothy 1:4b (CEB)

Let's continue with the questions that we began addressing in Chapter Five.

Question 4: What can go wrong, and how can I avoid the pitfalls that seem to trap me when I'm seeking God's will?
Answer: There are at least four areas that have potential pitfalls: how you read the Bible, how you pray, depending on doors being "opened" or "closed," and talking to other Christians.

Reading the Bible

Many of us follow a plan that sets out readings for each day. Imagine that right now you are reading the Book of Genesis, which recounts the life of Abraham and the miraculous things that happened to him. You read that Abraham talked with God, who told him to go to a new land. God also said that although Abraham

---

1 Paul is talking here about "certain individuals" who "spread wrong teaching" (1 Timothy 1:3 CEB).

127

and his wife were old, they would have a son. Later he was told to sacrifice the boy, but he was stopped by an angel who provided a sacrificial goat for the offering. (See Genesis 12, 18 and 22 NIV.)

You might wonder, "Could this happen to me? Would I actually hear God speak to me? Could God's direction in my life be that straightforward and clear?"

Biblical stories about the heroes of our faith, like Abraham, offer fundamental truths about how to live. They provide wisdom and encouragement, but they do not set the pattern for us. You should not expect the things that happened to Abraham will happen to you, and therefore theology professors say Abraham's experiences are not "normative." This means that you will not talk directly with God like Abraham. Nor will many other things in the Bible happen to you in the same way. For example, God will not speak to you from a burning bush (like Moses in Exodus 3); He will not send a prophet to anoint you as king (like David in First Samuel 16); and you will not see a blinding light and hear God's voice (like Paul in Acts 9).

You might wonder, "If the same things won't happen to me, why are those stories in the Bible?" They are there because of the lessons we can learn from them. In Abraham's story, for example, one lesson is that we can trust God even when things seem impossible. Although the underlying lesson will always be true (you can trust God no matter how impossible things seem), the miraculous method by which it happened (or the "how"— actually hearing God's voice) will not be the same. Thus, if you mistakenly wait to hear the voice of God based on the Abraham narrative, you will become frustrated by the sounds of silence.

Let me give another example of what can go wrong when you seek God's wisdom based on these stories. Think about the Book of Jonah, which tells the story of a man who was swallowed by a big fish. It has been used as an example of how to go about finding God's will. But ask yourself what this story is really all about.

Notice that Jonah was first told by God exactly where he should go and what he should do (to Nineveh in the east to preach). Instead, he disobeyed God and went in the opposite direction (to Tarshish in the west, planning to hide). The boat taking him to

Tarshish was hit by a storm, and Jonah was thrown into the water by the crew where he was swallowed by a large fish. After three days Jonah was vomited onto the shore. It was only then that Jonah went to Nineveh to preach to the people, which God had already plainly told him he should do.

It is clear that this story does not teach anything about finding the will of God. It is about disobedience and second chances, not about God's guidance. Its message could be, "Don't run from God," or, "If at first you fail to follow God's direction and go the wrong way, you can later repent and turn back to Him." Since Jonah already knew exactly what God wanted him to do, the story cannot be about finding God's will.

It is easy to get caught up in the details of the Bible's stories, and unless you think carefully about what you are studying, you can become confused. Even pastors can contribute to this confusion if they are not careful to explain Scripture thoroughly.[2]

There is another trap that is easy to fall into. When looking for an answer, you might decide to read the Bible selectively, focusing on verses you randomly find. Have you heard this joke about a person who was reading the Bible in that way? He first opened it and read, "So Judas threw the money into the temple and left. Then he went away and hanged himself" (Matthew 27:5 NIV). Not sure what to think, he randomly opened it to another page where he read, "Go and do likewise" (Luke 10:37 NIV). The point is, you should not look in the Bible randomly seeking verses that would tell you what to do.

I tried reading the Bible looking for a specific verse to tell me what to do only once. My wife and I were living in Colorado Springs, and we were in our late twenties with a three-year-old son and a dog. Our little boy would frequently play too rough with the dog, chasing him around the house. After a couple of months of this and with another baby on the way, we decided that we might have to rehome our dog.

---

2 Take a look at Karl Vaters' article, "Finding God's Will for Your Life Is Easier than You Think," in *Christianity Today*, found at https://www.christianitytoday.com/karl-vaters/2016/september/finding-gods-will-for-your-life-is-easier-than-you-think.html?paging=off. I also once heard a well-known preacher say, "You wouldn't be alive today unless God had something great in front of you." In a sense this is true, but that statement overlooks the fact that many people die or are injured every day because we live in a fallen world and are suffering because there is evil in the world.

We ran an ad in the newspaper, and some people came to the house. While they were getting to know our dog, we began to feel terrible about what we were doing. I began to randomly open the Bible, looking for something that might help. I turned to page after page and read a verse here and there, but I didn't find anything that came close to helping me with that decision. But I am glad to say that we decided not to rehome our dog, who lived with us for seventeen years!

Instead of jumping from one random verse to another, read each verse in the context of the rest of the passage, of the book you are reading, and of the entire biblical text.[3] If you are already following a Bible-reading plan, then continue as scheduled, for there is no better way to find God's wisdom.

The Bible provides us with insight into the character and nature of God, and it is a miraculous book. Read it. Study it. Rely on it. I have made it a practice to read it through each year.[4] I find it fresh and new every day, and I think you would, too. But don't count on being able to open it and find a verse that will tell you what to do.

Prayer

Let's consider the role that prayer plays in helping to find God's will. The followers of other world religions believe that their gods are distant and unknowable, and they have no way to communicate with them. But Christians know that God is personal and fully known and revealed through Jesus Christ. Hence, they can communicate directly with God through prayer.

Prayer is a powerful gift from God assuring us that He is present and active. We understand that prayer is commanded for all believers and is helpful in all circumstances. Paul encourages us to "pray continually" (1 Thessalonians 5:17 NIV), and James says, "The prayer of a righteous person is powerful and effective" (James 5:16b NIV). When faced with a big decision, you might pray for specific guidance. It is possible you will receive an unmistakable answer, but what if you do not?

---

3 Robert H. Stein, *A Basic Guide to Interpreting the Bible* (Grand Rapids, Michigan: Baker Books, 1994), 57, 166.
4 Richard J. Foster, *Celebration of Discipline: The Path to Spiritual Growth* (New York: HarperCollins Publishers, 1978, 1988, 1998).

I have only had one prayer answered so immediately and directly that I understood it to be a clear and immediate response from God. I had been praying about an issue for some time and finally asked God for an unmistakable sign to resolve the matter. The very next day I was unable to read or understand what people were saying, and I was diagnosed as having a stroke.

With my wife out of town, I was taken to the hospital in my first ever ambulance ride and admitted for a couple of days. A later diagnosis concluded that I had experienced a TIA (transient ischemic attack), but finally a few months later it was determined to have been a migraine headache without pain. There was no long-term injury, and I did receive what I consider to be an unmistakable answer, but I no longer pray in that way.

What if God is silent or provides an answer that seems to be ambiguous? What if you believe you heard one response today and something different tomorrow? Since we are to pray at all times, how does praying more fervently lead to a better answer when you are in the midst of making a decision than at other times? And what does all of this say about your prayer in the routine times? Instead, simply pray for wisdom, guidance and direction.

Open or Closed Doors
There are times when a particular path is either available or not, for one reason or another. For example, what if some years after taking your initial job and getting married, you receive an unsolicited job offer from a new employer in a different state. You might consider this to be an open door to change jobs, but now imagine that you and your spouse have children, so your family would also have to relocate. This means your children would have to change schools and your spouse would have to move with you and change jobs. What if one person thinks the door is open, while the other thinks any door requiring a move should be considered closed? Which door would be open? How could you determine when a door is open and when it is closed? My suggestion is, don't be concerned with this.

Talking with Other Christians

You should be in fellowship with other Christians because, when faced with a difficult decision, you can talk to them about what to do. You might seek the advice of four of your Christian friends about a potential job change. You think it might be best to remain in your current job, which is in a comfortable setting near your family and friends. Three of your friends agree, but one has a different opinion. Which advice should you follow? Could you be getting conflicting advice because of the way you asked the question? Or could your three friends subconsciously be looking at it from a selfish point of view, hoping to keep you nearby?

Paul was faced with a similar situation in the Book of Acts. He was in Caesarea on his way to Jerusalem when he encountered Agabus, a prophet who did not believe that Paul should continue his trip. Agabus took Paul's belt and with it he tied his hands and feet, saying the Holy Spirit had told him,

> *"... 'In this way the Jewish leaders in Jerusalem will bind the owner of this belt and will hand him over to the Gentiles.'" When we heard this, we and the people there pleaded with Paul not to go up to Jerusalem* (Acts 21:11–12 NIV).

What did Paul do? Did he follow the advice of this well-meaning prophet and his friends? No. Paul considered what he had been told but nonetheless decided to continue his trip to Jerusalem.

This story highlights how difficult it can be to know which of your friends is correct. And what if your friends all agree on one course of action, but, like Paul, you don't? You could be right and all your contrary advisors wrong; or they might be right and you could be wrong. This rarely helps clarify the search for God's will.

Question 5: What role do small things play in experiencing God's will?

Answer: There is nothing small that happens in our lives. What may seem "small" at the time may, in retrospect, turn out to be of great importance later in life. I have experienced this throughout my life.

Example 1

After I completed my active military service obligation, I became a member of the Air Force reserves. To receive retirement pay, my service would have to exceed twenty years, and in order to get that many years, I had to be promoted from Major to Lt. Colonel. But I wasn't optimistic about getting promoted because I had not completed the classes strongly recommended to reach that level. When the promotion list was announced, I was shocked to see my name was on it, and I could not imagine how it happened.

A few years later I ran into one of my Air Force friends from my first assignment. After some small talk he said, "I'll bet you are wondering how you got your last promotion." I didn't know what he was getting at, but said, "Yeah, I've always wondered how that happened since I didn't have the courses typically required." That is when he told me that he had been the head of my promotion board, and when he saw my name, he took a close look at my record. He recognized that even without the courses I deserved to be promoted. Without his interest it would have been difficult for me to be promoted, and my service would have ended short of the required twenty years with no retirement pay.

That small event did not happen by chance, and it was not a lucky accident. Instead, God was ensuring things worked for good in my life. How else could it have happened that of the hundreds of officers up for promotion, the head of my board would be an officer who took a particular interest in my record? What had seemed like a small detail turned out to have very big implications later.

Example 2

My son and I participated in a wilderness experience in California that was very challenging. It was an experience to remember. After we got back, I told virtually everyone I knew about the trip, and I was scheduled to make a presentation in some of the Sunday school classes at our church. As part of that, I thought I might be able to arrange for one of the leaders of the camping program to make a visit to West Virginia and help me with advertising. Not knowing anyone to call, though, I phoned the office in California and started talking to the lady who answered the phone. I told her that I thought it would be great if someone could come to West Virginia to help me spread the word. When I finished, she was pretty quiet and then slowly said she had just finished praying for a way to reach out to others about their program. And that's when I called. She said that she would be happy to come and help.

She arrived, and my wife and kids really liked her, especially our daughter. We did all we could to inform others about the program, but ultimately it did not have much impact. However, she told me about a new ministry that had just started in Boulder, Colorado, called Promise Keepers. She said that during the coming summer they would be holding another event in Indianapolis, but it was sold out. I called around (this was before the days of the internet) to see if I could find tickets for me and my son. A few calls later I located a man in Iowa who had tickets for a large group, and he had two more tickets than they needed.

We attended the conference with more than 70,000 other men, and it was a marvelous experience and time of growth. When I got back home a couple of days later, my life had changed as I felt compelled to make a difference for the Lord. I realized that the "small thing" of calling the wilderness ministry for assistance turned out to be significant in unanticipated ways.

> Heavenly Father,
> Help us to realize that there are no small things in our lives. Allow us to see that as long as our ambitions, goals and purposes are in agreement with Yours, everything in our lives will work together to bring You glory. Sometimes we think we are missing the mark because we are too shortsighted to see what You are aiming at. Our efforts are of no value unless they are grounded in You and the advance of Your kingdom. Bring us to the end of our self-sufficiency; increase our dependence on You and You alone. Change our doubts into times of confidence and trust, and let us never forget that You are with us always, to the end of the age.
> In Jesus' name, amen.

Chapter Thirteen

THE CHOICE IS YOURS

No eye has seen, no ear has heard, and no mind has imagined what God has prepared for those who love him.
—1 Corinthians 2:9 (NLT)

It had been a routine flight from JFK in New York to Miami for the 176 people aboard Eastern Airline's flight #401 on Friday night, December 29, 1972. As the airplane was approaching the runway for landing, the pilot attempted to lower the landing gear. But the light that should have come on in the cockpit indicating that the wheels had locked into place did not illuminate. There was no way to determine whether it was safe, so the captain aborted the landing and began circling over a deserted part of the nearby Everglades while he assessed the problem.

It was possible to climb through an opening in the floor of the cockpit and conduct a visual inspection of the landing gear. The co-pilot left his position and began to investigate. Shortly thereafter the captain thought he better have a look as well, so he put the airplane on autopilot and also headed below. Unnoticed by the pilot, however, his leg bumped the controls as he got up and disengaged the autopilot.

The plane began a very slow, imperceptible descent of a few feet each second. Because they were flying over the darkness of the swamp, there were no ground lights or other points of reference to alert anyone that the plane was slowly descending. Four minutes later the plane flew at full speed into the ground, killing more than a hundred passengers. When it crashed, no one was flying the plane!

It is easy to get caught up in the details of life and overlook the big picture, the things that are of critical importance. Don't let that happen to you. This book attempts to help with one of the most important aspects of your life: experiencing God's will.

Some people think experiencing God's will requires that they discover and stay on God's Plan A for their lives. They imagine it to be like having to successfully walk on a tightrope across a large, deep gorge. The thought of doing this fills them with fear as they hesitate to even take the first step.

Imagine that you must walk this tightrope. Could you do it?

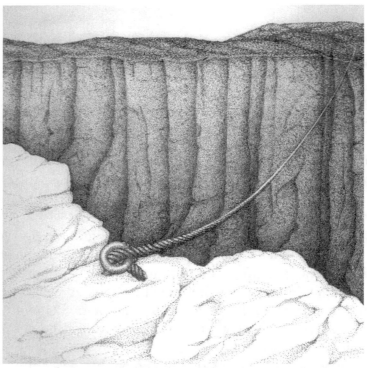

This drawing is by Cheryl Alison of Worcester, Massachusetts.

God, however, does not require that you stay on a preselected path known only to Him. As Jesus taught us in the Book of Matthew:

> *Don't bargain with God. Be direct. Ask for what you need. **This isn't a cat-and-mouse, hide-and-seek game we're in.** If your child asks for bread, do you trick him with sawdust? If he asks for fish, do you scare him with a live snake on his plate? As bad as you are, you wouldn't think of such a thing. You're at least decent to your own children. So don't you think the God who conceived you in love will be even better?* (Matthew 7:7–11 MSG, emphasis added).

Don't fall into the trap of thinking you must walk a tightrope to experience God's will.

Instead, you can follow the Path of Assurance, which teaches that as you delight yourself in the Lord, the desires of your heart become aligned with His. God will then work things together for good while transforming you to the image of His Son. Don't mistake this grand plan for simply a way to make decisions about the details of life. In Colossians 3:1–2 (MSG), Paul says,

> *So if you're serious about living this new resurrection life with Christ, act like it. Pursue the things over which Christ presides. Don't shuffle along, eyes to the ground, absorbed with the things right in front of you. Look up, and be alert to what is going on around Christ—that's where the action is. See things from his perspective.*

God's will is not focused on your next job, or where you live, or other details of your life. Decisions about those things can be made using your God-given good judgment and common sense. God has provided you with gifts of reasoning and free will, so whatever specific path you choose, you can trust that He will work it for good. It is not critical how or where you serve Him—just that you do it! Sometimes you may feel God's presence and peace with a decision, but not always.

Instead of trying to walk a tightrope, God's will can be better understood as a fountain with water gushing out in all directions into a surrounding pool. Imagine that each of your decisions is represented by one drop in that pool. Whatever trajectory the water drop takes as it leaves the fountain, it falls within the pool. It would look more like this:

Let me ask you this: Is the tightrope or the flowing fountain more consistent with the wide-open, spacious life God has promised? Experiencing God's will is like the fountain with its flowing water. With it you have the freedom to confidently make decisions, big and small, without fear of making the wrong one.

Instead of walking a tightrope, live in the shower of God's immense love. God cares about the details of your everyday life, but He gives you the freedom to make decisions. You don't have to worry about the next step. Have confidence that He who began a good work in you will see it through to completion. To again paraphrase Ron Hutchcraft, if you know the planner, you don't need to be concerned about the plan.[1]

There is no need to wait for a supernatural sign, or for your friends to agree on what is best, or anything else. Instead, it is up to you to act, using your best judgment. Then trust God to work things for good. Your discernment is a precious gift from a loving God—use it. Reach beyond what you can grasp and open your heart and mind to the magnificence of a loving Father who only wants the best for you.

When you are faced with one of life's frequent and inevitable decisions, don't be afraid, thinking that you have to toe the line to avoid falling. Instead, look at the situation, make the best decision you can, and then move on. You can count on being in the pool of God's will as you make any God-honoring decision. As you make the choice to move from a life filled with fear toward a life that is full and free, give God praise and honor.

God's will for your life can probably best be summarized in this statement attributed to St. Augustine: "Love God, and do what you want."[2] Always expect the best.

The End of Our Life on Earth and the Beginning of a Whole New World

While at Moody we were taught that if the Bible told us much more about heaven, then we would be so excited about getting there that we would be consumed by it. The Bible provides only

---

1 Ron Hutchcraft Ministries, Inc., *2021 Calendar – February* (Harrison, Arizona, 2020).
2 The full quote is, "Love God and do whatever you please: for the soul trained in love to God will do nothing to offend the One who is Beloved" (Dr. Bill Strom, "Love God, and Do What You Will," *The Life*, April 2, 2019, https://thelife.com/devotionals/love-god-and-do-what-you-will).

a few brief descriptions of what heaven will be like. Consider this from the apostle Paul:

> *For instance, we know that when these bodies of ours are taken down like tents and folded away, they will be replaced by resurrection bodies in heaven—God-made, not handmade—and we'll never have to relocate our "tents" again. Sometimes we can hardly wait to move— and so we cry out in frustration. Compared to what's coming, living conditions around here seem like a stop- over in an unfurnished shack, and we're tired of it! We've been given a glimpse of the real thing, our true home, our resurrection bodies! The Spirit of God whets our appetite by giving us a taste of what's ahead. He puts a little of heaven in our hearts so that we'll never settle for less* (2 Corinthians 5:1–5 MSG).

Heaven will be spectacular in every respect. Think of it, there will be no more tears or sorrow, no more pain or suffering, and no more hearing aids or glasses! One of the most difficult things to imagine is that there will be no more time as we understand it because we will be living in eternity. Imagine a life with no watches or alarm clocks and where you can't be late for a meet- ing. Right now much of your life is governed by time as you move through expected routines: sleep, meals, work, holidays, birthdays, etc. Time here is limited by the very calendars that will disappear in heaven. It is impossible to imagine what life will be like without those markers. Try to grasp the promise of living in that environment forever.

Why are many of us so scared of death? Could it be fear of the unknown? Could it be doubt that heaven is really too good to be true? While here on earth we spend money to preserve the appearance of youth, even though it will inevitably fade. First there are your golden years, then the sunset years and finally no more years on this earth. The great and the small will face that same moment when this life ends, and all of your accom- plishments will be of little consequence. Then we will be fully engulfed by God's gracious goodness as our new life begins. Do not fear this transformation when it comes.

When my mother was near the end of her life on earth, she said something that has stuck with me. She was talking about how she was feeling when she suddenly said, "I never knew it would be so hard to die. But I am ready." She was a godly woman who had lived her life to glorify God and was frustrated by how long she was living in what had become her broken and sick body. Rather than fearing what was next, however, she was ready to welcome it and was sure it would be a wonderful blessing. Do you have that mindset as the end of this life approaches? When you think about the end of your earthly existence, you should always keep your mind fixed on what awaits.

In 2013 my wife and I attended a conference at The Cove, the Billy Graham conference center near Montreat, North Carolina, to hear Ken Boa speak[3]. A brilliant man, Ken told us a hypothetical story about twin babies living in their mother's womb before birth. They were somehow able to communicate with each other and did not yet have any idea of what life after birth would be like. One of their conversations might have gone something like this:

Baby 1: "I think we might be getting out of here soon. I'm not sure what's coming next, but it's dark here, and things are getting a little cramped. I need more, so let's move on."

Baby 2: "Not me. This is the life for me. I don't need a thing. I have all I want to eat, and I don't have to work at all, not even to breathe. I like the comfort of floating around in here and am perfectly comfortable right now. I don't want to go anywhere. And besides, who knows if the rumors we hear of the next life are even true? Do you think they are, or will all this just come to an end?"

Baby 1: "I don't know, but if there really is a next life, what do you think it will be like? Where would

3 "God of Wonders: The Creator and His Handiwork," a conference held at the Billy Graham Training Center at The Cove, led by Ken Boa, September 20-22, 2013.

we go anyway, how could there be room for all of us, and how could it be any better than this?"

Baby 2: "I just can't imagine it, but I'm scared and not sure what to believe. So I have decided to stay right here."

Then they were born, and the babies enjoyed beautiful sights, wonderful sounds, delicious food and many other things that are a part of life here on earth. Still, it must have been scary when they were born and left what was comfortable. So scary, in fact, that they almost certainly started off crying! But as they grew, they experienced lives that were incredibly richer. We have similar questions about the next life: is it really true, will there be room for everyone, what will we do throughout eternity, and will it be better than what we have in this life?

What will it be like? There is a whole new world out there—one that is even more dazzling, exciting and incredible than anything you can imagine. If you keep your focus on that, then the difficulties you are facing and the decisions you make now will all stay in their proper perspective.

As you enter fully into the plan God has for you, your life will never be the same. You are blessed to be a blessing. Now get to it!

Dear Lord,

As we conclude this book, we ask You to fill us with a desire to serve You more fully and to grasp how to do it in a way that brings glory to Your name. Take away our self-confidence and fill us with reliance on You. Help us to know that Your plan for us is to grow in trusting faith in Your mercy and grace through Your Son. Free us from the fear and worry that we might miss Your plan for our lives. We know that You have provided us with an open and spacious life to enjoy and live to the fullest. We know that Your ways and thoughts are far above our own, and so we can trust You to work all things together for good.

Keep our eyes open to see signs of Your presence all around us and to live a happy and rewarding life. Don't allow us to reduce Jesus to what we are, but instead let Him raise us to all that we can be through Him. We pray that You will give us confidence and trust to allow us to do things, to meet people and to take risks in our lives, confident that we always will be in Your care and plan for our lives. We thank You that we are not walking on a tightrope afraid to take the next step. Instead, we know that Your plan is more abundant, complex and wonderful than anything we can ask or think. And so we move forward in the confident hope that You, who began a good work in us, will carry it through to completion.

In Jesus' name we pray, amen.